AROUND *the* TABLE

WILLIAM MORROW
An Imprint of HarperCollins Publishers

AROUND
the
TABLE

Recipes *and* Inspiration

for Gatherings Throughout *the* Year

Martina McBride

WITH KATHERINE COBBS

HarperCollins books may be purchased for educational, business, or sales promotional use. For information please e-mail the Special Markets Department at SPsales@harpercollins.com.

FIRST EDITION

Designed by Pagnozzi Creative
Photographs © by Jason Wallis

Library of Congress Cataloging-in-Publication Data has been applied for.

ISBN 978-0-06-232391-0 (hardcover)
ISBN 978-0-06-237716-6 (B&N signed edition)

14   15   16   17   18   ID6/QG   10   9   8   7   6   5   4   3   2   1

To all the friends and family
who have graced my home and spent so many
hours laughing and loving here.

To John, Delaney, Emma, and Ava,
who are always so sweet and appreciative
of my cooking. The times we've shared around
the table are some of my favorite memories.

For Flavia McBride, who was
an inspiration to me in countless ways.
I was especially inspired by her passion
for cooking and entertaining. She made
everyone feel welcome and loved.

Contents

Author's Note

The meals in my house growing up were not the stuff of today's food magazines or shows. They were midwestern and very simple—casseroles, Salisbury steak, hamburgers, boiled or mashed potatoes, peas, green beans . . . and Pineapple Upside-Down Cake, Peach Cobbler, and Strawberry Shortcake were our dessert standards. We had instant iced tea at every meal and coffee was Taster's Choice or Folger's. While I have experienced a lot of different foods and flavors in my life and travels, I remember those meals around my family's table during the '70s and '80s fondly.

We all hang on to things from childhood, and food memories, especially, become so much a part of who we are. Cooking for and hosting family and friends regularly is one way I try to create lasting memories for my girls, too. I find comfort in knowing that even when my girls are away from home, they will long for my pot roast (a recipe handed down from my mom). And one day I know the phone will ring and it will be one of them asking me how to make it for their family.

If I weren't a performer, I think I would love to be a party planner. Every aspect of planning a gathering—coming up with the party theme, designing a unique invitation, creating a menu, and setting the scene—speaks to my creative side. For me, a party is a gift for my friends and family. My goal is to make each person feel special from the moment they receive the invitation until they walk out my door. If there is one thing I want to impress upon you with this book, it's to not let the idea of throwing a party be intimidating. Successful gatherings don't have to be elaborate or expensive. Your generosity and the thought and effort you put into the details are key to making guests feel welcome and appreciated. If they leave feeling that way, then you've succeeded. And if a farm girl from Kansas can do it, anyone can!

As a daughter, sister, mother, wife, and friend, I gear my party-planning advice and ideas to everyone, even beginners. Over the years, I've developed a system that really works for me. I get inspiration from lots of places—TV shows, magazines, books, blogs, the changing seasons, and friends—and I am always on the lookout for fresh ideas or twists on traditional themes.

I wanted to create a scrapbook of my parties and recipes to share with my girls and that's how this book came to be. I hope it inspires you, too. I don't believe there is such a thing as "effortless" entertaining. Parties take planning and organization (not my best skills, by the way), but with practice and the tools found in this book, entertaining can *look* effortless. If you've never played host, start simple with a party like Family Pizza Night (page 80) or Fall Supper with Friends (page 23). As you gain experience, you can throw more elaborate parties with confidence.

The reasons to host a party are all around you. Do it to celebrate those you care about. Do it when the seasons change. Do it to try out that recipe that looked so delicious on Pinterest. Do it for the fun you'll create and, most of all, the memories you'll make. Do it just because!

—*Martina*

HOW TO USE THIS BOOK

I've been entertaining for years now, and I have a lot more confidence in the kitchen these days than when I was first hosting. I also have spent many hours on a tour bus or cozied up on my couch at home poring through cookbooks and entertaining books—it's how I unwind! Whenever I come across a new recipe, ingredient, or a different take on an old favorite that inspires me, I find a way to add it to the menu for my next party. I have learned so much about food, style, and being a good hostess from these resources and from trial and error in the kitchen.

The parties in this book represent the many different sides of my life. I'm a mom who loves having my family together for a warm Spring Brunch Outdoors or a colorful Taco Fiesta. I'm a wife who relishes an opportunity to get a bit glam and serve up a Retro Valentine's Day menu for my husband. I am a singer and entertainer who has had a lifelong love affair with music and enjoys an evening of good wine, good company, good tunes, and good food from my Red Wine and Vinyl party menu. I'm a loyal friend who counts my blessings for the amazing people in my life and will find any excuse to celebrate them over brunch. And I'll always be a girl from Kansas who willingly serves up Dad's crowd-pleasing potato salad and Mom's peach cobbler to a boisterous crowd on the 4th of July. These parties were inspired by friends (Bountiful Tuscan Feast), travels (Taco Fiesta), being on the road (Bruschetta Bash), the seasons, and holidays (Mistletoe and Martinis). I find inspiration everywhere! The menus include prized recipes from my family and friends, along with new favorites, and suggestions for embellishing store-bought ingredients when you don't feel like doing all the cooking.

No matter your experience, the parties in this book can be adapted to fit your own comfort level and your style. Each party comes with a suggested menu, but please feel free to pare down the list of recipes to suit your crowd, your comfort level, and your timing. I wanted to give you some bang for your buck, so I share a lot of recipes here. If you decide to prepare all of the recipes from a party's menu, I have provided you with a step-by-step game plan so you can stay sane and organized. Otherwise, pick and choose your favorites from the list and start cooking! You can even mix and match menus. One thing I want to stress is that this is *your* party—once you decide to host it—not my party. So if I list two appetizers and you only want to make one, that's totally fine. If whiskey isn't your thing, change up the cocktail to whatever you like or offer your favorite beer or nonalcoholic drink.

To help you get started, I've included my tips for entertaining on a budget, creating unique invitations, decorating ideas that can be dialed up or kept simple, fun favors, and "sanity savers": my tried-and-true tips for relieving you of unnecessary party stress. Each party's game plan will help take the guesswork out of getting ready so you can stay organized every step of the way. I share photos and stories from the parties I've thrown to inspire and guide you.

Remember, this book is meant to get you excited about entertaining, so feel free to improvise and incorporate your own ideas to make these parties your own.

Introduction

GET THE HOSTING STARTED!

Entertaining at home is something I wish people would do more often. It doesn't have to be overwhelming or intimidating. I'm a big believer in starting small before moving on to more complicated parties. Experience is the best teacher and it takes time to find your comfort zone. There are so many ways to entertain—from hosting a small casual supper to throwing a formal seated dinner or large cocktail party—so it's important not only to be familiar with your space, style, and budget, but also your ability to juggle tasks and your threshold for handling the unexpected. You can translate that knowledge into a party setup that works best for you. One of my favorite ways to entertain involves just putting on a big pot of soup and serving it with a loaf of crusty bread. It can truly be that simple. I say this a lot: planning is key! It is the secret to a relaxed host—and a relaxed host means relaxed guests.

BE INSPIRED

Holidays, birthdays, promotions, a new house, and a new baby are regular occasions that inspire celebrations. But I look for inspiration in other places, too. The change of seasons is a big one for me. I like to celebrate each one by building a menu around what's growing at a particular time of year and decorating the table with seasonal finds—pumpkins in autumn or farmers' market produce in summer, for instance. I urge you to start by opening your home to friends and family just four times a year, once each season, to get in the habit of hosting regular gatherings.

I love to settle in with a cup of coffee and a recipe book or magazine and dream up the next party I might throw. Sometimes I will be spontaneous and have friends over just because, and that's when it pays to have a few staples on hand: nuts, salami, cheese, crackers, a couple bottles of wine (see The Party Pantry, page 11). You don't have to have fancy stuff to have fun. Other times, I might crave a margarita, so I figure why not invite my favorite people over to share a pitcher of margaritas over a casual taco supper? Every party doesn't have to start with a save-the-date card followed by a formal invitation. There is no one "right" way to throw a party. Find one that works best for you.

VISUALIZE THE SETUP

Once you've decided to go for it and throw a party, imagine the scene playing out. Is it going to be a seated dinner or a heavy hors d'oeuvres affair? It's important to decide how you want to serve the food and drinks. Do you want a family-style dinner where guests pass platters of food around the table and serve themselves? Or does it make more sense to set up a casual buffet and let guests eat from plates on their laps? This decision is as important as, or maybe more important than, any other because it dictates your menu, your serving dishes, the party flow, and its overall vibe. Set out all the serving pieces you think you'll need—platters, bowls, trays, and utensils—and label the use for each with a Post-it note. Make a list of any pieces you need to borrow or purchase so you're not scrambling for a dish the day of the party.

The invitation reads:

PLEASE JOIN MARTINA AND JOHN FOR

DRINKS
& "DISH"

SATURDAY, OCTOBER 30TH, 2010
AT 6:30 P.M.

THINK OUTSIDE THE ENVELOPE

With a party vision in place, it's time to spread the word. E-mailed invitations are okay, especially for a large group, but old-fashioned snail mail invitations are special. It's always exciting to get an invitation in the mail. The most important thing is that your intended guests actually get invited, so don't stress out if you don't have time to design, print, and mail invitations. But if you do have the time and desire, remember that it's important that the look of the invitation fits your occasion. For example, if you are giving a casual backyard barbecue, you wouldn't want to send an engraved invitation that screams "FORMAL!" and vice versa.

It's also fun to think outside the envelope! Once when I hosted a Mexican dinner, I wrote the party details in gold paint pen on poblanos and red bell peppers, put them in a small box, and hand-delivered them to my guests. It was unexpected and let them know right from the start that it was going to be a festive and fun evening.

The information on your invitation is important. Obviously it should include the date, time, and place. But it's also helpful to say a little bit about the occasion or theme, even naming your party as I did with the parties in this book. Optional, but extremely helpful to your guests, is defining the dress code. Usually the party theme makes what to wear relatively clear, but if there is a specific way you want your guests to dress—black tie, cocktail dress, or business attire—state it clearly on the invite. If it truly doesn't matter, "casual" is pretty much understood by all.

FAN OF A PLAN

The key to pulling off a great gathering is organization, organization, organization! You will be more at ease if you plan ahead and make all the advance preparations.

I am a firm believer in lists. I love lists. I make lists so I can cross stuff off as I do it. It's so satisfying. And I go old-school with pen and paper. I find if I write something down I actually remember it better. You need shopping lists, to-do lists, what-to-make-ahead lists, what-dishes-are-you-going-to-use lists, and timing-of-the-party lists. Just remember, everything always takes a little longer than you think it will! (FYI: It's important to put "shower and get ready" on your list. Many times I've still been in the kitchen, no makeup and my hair up in a bun, thirty minutes before guests arrive!)

As I've said, I don't believe there is such a thing as effortless entertaining. The key is to make hosting a party *look* effortless. That comes from all the planning and preparation you do. It really does pay off.

When it comes to menus for entertaining, I like to choose one showstopper recipe and pair it with simpler, harmonious ones. And I'm a fan of seasonal dishes and ingredients. It's hard to get excited about eating chili when it's 100 degrees outside. (Well, unless you're my husband. He will eat chili anytime!) I love how Europeans are inspired to cook whatever is fresh at the market on a given day, which usually comes from nearby farms and gardens. They let the ingredients inspire the menu. I do the same whenever possible.

For entertaining, it's always helpful to plan a menu with mostly recipes you can make ahead of time. Or at least recipes you can prep ahead of time. I believe you should stick with what you do best. If baking isn't your strong suit (um . . . that would be me), it's okay to serve a simple dessert like fresh berries and whipped cream or ice cream jazzed up with a warm chocolate sauce instead of making a soufflé! There is absolutely nothing wrong with picking up a beautiful cake from the local bakery—or, quite frankly, as much of the menu as you'd like, if it enables you to have people over with less stress. If you plan to halve or double a recipe, take the time to write it down with the new measurements. It's easy to get in the middle of a recipe and forget that you are changing it.

LESS IS OFTEN BEST

It only takes a little bit of effort to make a gathering feel special. Whether it's a creative invitation, a beautiful place setting, a unique cocktail, fresh flowers and candlelight, or music that matches the party mood or theme, you want your guests to feel that you have put some thought into the occasion and that you really want them there.

Sure, it's nice to have your house look pretty with great food and tasty drinks on display, but nobody enjoys a stuffy party where everything is perfect but the host is stressed-out and miserable. It's the laughter and love that everyone will remember long after the party ends. As host, you set the tone for the party, and it's your job to put everyone at ease.

It's human nature to want everything to be perfect when you entertain. Well, I'm here to tell you that achieving perfection is rare, so just take a deep breath, laugh, and go with it. One time I had my band and crew over for a holiday party and I made a big pot of jambalaya. I thought I'd made plenty to eat. But, apparently, everyone was really hungry, and I ran out of food! I could have been mortified and let stress ruin the party,

but luckily I had a few frozen pizzas in my freezer. I popped those in and just went with it. The party didn't miss a beat. Everyone was having a great time and no one went home hungry. My advice: just go with the flow! And perhaps you should always have a few pizzas in your freezer!

It helps to think ahead. If you have something precious that you don't want knocked over and broken, put it away for the party. If you have white furniture and you are obsessed with no stains or spills, don't serve red wine (there *will* be spills, trust me). If you have a pet that gets nervous around people, let him spend the night with someone you trust or put him in a comfortable place. Actually, I would vote to always put pets away during gatherings. I love animals, but not all guests are comfortable with a dog getting to know them or jumping up on their new dress, and people tend to want to feed your pets all kinds of tasty treats that aren't good for them.

SET THE SCENE

Setting a mood and decorating to create a vibe is one of my favorite parts of prepping for a party. Stand in your living room or dining room and take a good long look. Is it cluttered? Are there knickknacks on a shelf that are dusty and forgotten? Now imagine how you want your room to look: free of clutter . . . a pretty throw pillow on the couch . . . a lovely scented candle . . . a small vase of fresh roses . . . lights you can dim. Sometimes we get so used to a room that we forget to *see* it. And I'm not talking about breaking the bank to make these changes. Just a couple of small tweaks may help you feel so much better about having people over and enjoying your space. Simple things like fresh flowers and a pretty table setting go a long way toward creating a cozy atmosphere. I look for items when I am out shopping that I know I can use. Cool dishes, napkins, vases, and more. It's fun to find vintage pieces or dishes you can mix and match. Don't forget candles! Flickering flames add warmth to the table and ambience to any party. Always use unscented candles on the table or near the food. I either group short ivory pillar candles together or place tea lights in clear votive holders all around. Your table should glow. Plus, who doesn't look better by candlelight?

By the way, I have a secret for cleaning up clutter before people come to my house. It's called a big, deep drawer (and a closet) where I can stuff things and deal with them after the party. Under the bed is great for that, too. (This might just be the most practical advice in this entire book!)

TABLE SETTING 101

Unless you live *Downton Abbey*–style, setting a full-on formal table is probably a rarity. Still, it's great to know what a proper place setting looks like as well as what all those serving pieces are for. Maybe you inherited your grandmother's silver service and don't know a butter knife from a cheese spreader. Instead of leaving them in the silverware drawer, put them to use. The same goes for the formal china you got as a wedding gift or splurged on in a weak moment. Take it out of storage and use it—every day, even. Mix it up, too. Matchy-matchy gets boring. A place setting is like a party outfit, so create a table that reflects your style as well as the party.

A PLACE FOR EVERYONE

Place cards can be an element where you really express your creativity. I've used many different things such as autumn leaves from my yard, river rocks, and Polaroid pictures of guests as they arrive. I was at a dinner at Margrit Mondavi's (widow of winemaker Robert Mondavi) in the Napa Valley where she hand-painted each of our place cards with little lambs in watercolors. You can bet we each took them home as keepsakes! I've put a little present at each plate with the name of the guest on it and even a pretty miniature potted plant with the guest's name written directly on the pot. These become great favors to take home at the end of the evening. You can also invest in something that can be used over and over again. I bought mini chalkboards that make great reusable place cards with names written in chalk. I like to think about the seating arrangement and use place cards to mix things up a bit so that people interact and get to know each other better.

Think about your guests and their strengths. You don't want to put two very shy, quiet people next to each other. Put them by someone who will draw them out and include them in the conversation. By the same token if you have two talkative, vivacious, charming guests, consider spreading them out to keep conversation and the energy flowing and not concentrated all in one spot.

Likewise, don't let guests wander around with no direction. Bring them into the heart of the party, offer them a drink upon arrival, and take the time to chat with them for a bit or introduce them to another guest if you have to run off to check on something in the kitchen. When introducing guests who don't know one another, say something about each to serve as a conversation starter. Mention a common interest or tell a quick story. This gives them a jumping-off point and puts them at ease.

CURRYING FAVOR

It's always a nice touch to bring a gift for the hostess when you attend a party. Something as simple as a bottle of wine, extra-virgin olive oil, pretty hand soap, or good-quality coffee beans. So many ideas! I like to tailor the gift to the host's interests.

Though it's not necessary or expected, sometimes I like giving gifts or favors to guests at the end of the evening. They can be both place card and favor as mentioned before. But it's also nice to stick with the theme of your party. If you are having an Italian dinner, make extra red sauce and put it in jars with a recipe card tied to the lid. If you are doing a Valentine's Day dinner, snap a picture of each couple during dinner or as they arrive, then take a couple of minutes before the night ends to print them and put them in a little frame to give as a send-off. It's also nice to put something like this in the mail a few days later as a little memento of a great time spent together. This is just another place where you can get really creative and have some fun.

GOOD "GUESTIQUETTE"

Your job as a guest is to enjoy. You should compliment the host on something . . . and do so sincerely! Whether it's the food, the decor, or the music, share your appreciation for the work that was put into the party.

Circulate. Don't keep anyone trapped in conversation the whole night. This is not the place for intimate, deep conversation. If you find yourself talking about something in depth with another guest and you feel like it is keeping you both from the party, say, "I really want to talk to you about this more, but I don't want to be rude to the other guests. Let's get together soon and finish this conversation."

Offer to help, but don't belabor it. Some hosts welcome help while others are in plan-execution mode or just aren't good at delegating what needs to be done (um . . . again that would be me!) and would just rather do it themselves. Respect this. Offer your help once, and if your offer isn't accepted, just be available and attentive. If the host ever looks overwhelmed (or casts you a desperate look), then quietly offer to help out again; otherwise let them host.

And when it comes to cocktails, have fun, but don't overdo it. Enough said!

THE PARTY PANTRY FOR UNEXPECTED OCCASIONS

I think it's important to have a well-stocked pantry for unexpected guests—the sort of things that are shelf-stable that you can throw together in a heartbeat, like crackers for the cheese in your fridge, condiments for a relish tray, or a few sweets to go with tea or coffee. My go-to staples include:

Crackers and breadsticks, tortilla chips, pretzels, veggie chips, pita crisps

Cheese

Nuts

Pesto, tapenade, salsa, hummus

Pickles, olives

Dried fruit like apricots, dates, or plums, dried pasta, canned diced tomatoes

Dark chocolate, cookies, and biscotti

RAISE THE BAR

If you're serving wines with each course, appropriate stemware is preferred. But there is nothing wrong with serving wine in a pretty juice glass or an interesting tumbler. Stemless wine glasses are a great investment because they can be used for water and cocktails, too, and they aren't as fragile or tipsy as stemware.

It's a good idea to have a stash of beverages and mixers on hand so you always have a good variety to offer guests. I like to keep a few six-packs or bottles of these drinks on hand:

Sodas: Coca-Cola, Dr Pepper (my husband, John, is a DP addict), 7Up or Sprite, and ginger ale

Mixers: Seltzer water or club soda, tonic water, Bloody Mary mix

Juices: Cranberry, orange, apple, grapefruit, and lemonade or limeade

Coffee, tea bags, and cocoa

LIBATION CALCULATION

Obviously, you know your guests best, so feel free to increase or decrease these estimates. Also, take into consideration temperature. People will drink a lot more water outdoors in summer than at a seated dinner inside in December. Most caterers will tell you to count on two drinks per person for the first hour of the party and one drink each hour thereafter, so use this as a jumping-off point for what you'll need for your crowd. If you're serving a signature cocktail, take any mixers required into account and increase the calculation if you plan to serve nonalcoholic versions of the cocktail for nondrinkers. If nonalcoholic beverages are all you plan to serve, count on three to four drinks per guest. The calculations below are based upon a three-hour party. If you expect your party to last more than three hours, up the amounts accordingly.

Soft drinks: Three to four cans per guest

Mixers: Multiply the volume of mixer needed per cocktail
by 3 (for 3 drinks per person)

Water: One quart or liter per guest

Champagne: One (750 ml) bottle per guest
(4 glasses each)

Wine: One (750 ml) bottle per guest (4 glasses each)

Beer: Three to four (12-oz) bottles per guest

Liquor: Two (750 ml) bottles for every 8 guests
(3 or 4 cocktails per guest)

WINE AND FOOD PAIRING 101

Whether you drink a full-bodied Cab with fish tacos or Champagne with your chicken chili, as long as you enjoy what you're sipping there are no hard-and-fast rules. That said, below you will find some very general notes to keep in mind when it comes to wine pairing. Let the wine expert at your local store guide you when it comes to pairing wine with specific dishes. Pairing wine is like throwing parties . . . the more you do it, the better you'll get at it.

Bubbly—*Champagne, Prosecco, sparkling wine*
Pair with cheese, nuts, seafood, cured and smoked meats, creamy or buttery dishes, fruit desserts.

White—*Riesling (light-bodied, off-dry to sweet), Moscato (light-bodied, fruity efferves-cence), Sauvignon Blanc (medium-bodied, dry), Chardonnay (full-bodied, rich, oaked or unoaked)*
Lighter-bodied whites with a hint of sweetness pair well with spicy foods, boldly seasoned ethnic cuisine, cheese and charcuterie, and fruit desserts, while medium-bodied, drier whites are a great match with fresh cheeses, white meats, seafood, fresh herbs, vegetable dishes, and foods with a bit of sweetness. Full-bodied, buttery whites work with soft and aged cheeses, rich or creamy dishes, and shellfish, chicken, pork, and fatty fish.

Red—*Rosé (sweet or dry), Pinot Noir (light- to medium-bodied), Merlot (medium-bodied, fruity), Zinfandel (intense with berry notes), Malbec (bright, medium acidity), Cabernet Sauvignon (full-bodied, tannic)*
Red wine and red meat go together not because they share a common hue, but because the tannins that give red wine a slight bitter quality pair so well with the richness and fat of the meat. Hard cheeses like Parmigiano-Reggiano and Pecorino as well as aged blue-veined cheeses are other great matches for red wine.

party planning TIMELINE

THREE WEEKS AHEAD

- Create your guest list and call guests to check availability; it's good to find out if those you want to come are available so you can plan the date accordingly.

- Send out save-the-date cards or e-mails.

- Design the party invitation, clearly noting whether or not children are welcome. Set the start and finish times, so guests aren't still arriving after you've blown out the candles.

- Plan a stress-free menu with recipes that can be prepared ahead of time with most of the dishes being something you've made before.

- Plan what beverages you will offer. Juices, sparkling and still water, and red and white wine pretty much cover all bases when it comes to beverages, and they don't require a bartender for service. If you want to offer a signature cocktail or open bar, plan accordingly.

- Reserve party rentals such as chairs, linens, dishes, and flatware, if required. A good rule of thumb is two plates, forks, spoons, and glasses per guest. (Rental glasses are a time-saving splurge, since you simply rinse and return them.) Ask friends or family about borrowing items if you prefer.

- Book any help you require, such as a kitchen assistant, server, or bartender to help ease the workload. If you don't want to pay for a professional, enlist a neighbor's teenager, a niece or nephew, or a college kid. But remember, it's perfectly acceptable to offer your guests a tray to pass among themselves—plus it encourages mingling.

- Make a list of all nonperishables, decor, and setup items you need and buy or borrow any items you don't have on hand.

- Decide if you'll offer a parting gift now. Buy or make it and package it up as far in advance as possible.

TWO WEEKS AHEAD

- Mail or e-mail the party invitation.

- Create a shopping list for your menu, ideally organized by grocery aisle.

- Order any specialty foods, locally or online, that your menu requires.

- Create a chronological game plan noting how far in advance each dish or any of its components can be made ahead (and, if possible, frozen or refrigerated).

- Prepare freezable dishes and freeze them this week.

- Buy all beverages, calculating that you will need an average of 3 bottles of wine for every 4 people and/or 2 to 3 cocktails per guest for a two- to three-hour party. Keep wine in a cool, dark place out of direct heat and sunlight.

- Create a playlist of music to keep the party lively.

ONE WEEK AHEAD

- Clean any glassware, crystal, china, and silverware you'll be using.

- Wash and press all linens you'll be using.

- Decide which serving dishes you will use for each recipe and label each with a Post-it note to make sure you have all the dishes and utensils you need. Borrow or buy any extras you might need.

- Clean the house thoroughly now and maintain it so you only have to do touch-ups before the party.

THE DAY BEFORE THE PARTY

- Use your shopping list to purchase all perishable food items, including breads, produce, and dairy products.

- Refer to your lists and stage the party area.

- Make a bar station away from the dinner or buffet table and stock it with glasses, bowls for garnishes, napkins, shakers, jiggers, a bowl or bucket to keep white wine and/or Champagne chilled, and a bottle and wine opener.

- Tuck away items that will be in the way or precious items that might get broken.

- Arrange centerpieces, candles, and any other decorations. If it's a sit-down meal, go ahead and set your table. If it's a buffet, set it up, putting out the dishes, glasses, and utensils you will use to ensure you have ample space on the buffet.

- If it's rainy or cold, designate a place for coats in a closet near the entry, on a bed in a nearby room, or use an inexpensive portable garment rack. Even a bench near the door is better than guests holding their coats or draping them all over the house.

- Look to your game plan and do as much cooking and prep now as possible. If there is something you plan to (or have to) make the day-of, then chop and prep all the ingredients you possibly can now.

- Give your house a final once-over: De-clutter and tidy up wherever needed.

- Make a final, thorough to-do list for party day. Walk through the party in your mind. Take time to write down every detail. You will inevitably forget something. It happens to all of us. More than once I have opened the refrigerator the day after a party to see a whole platter or bowl of food I forgot to put out! A detailed to-do list forces you to think through each step and visualize what needs to be done.

THE DAY OF THE PARTY

- Final touches: Make sure bathrooms are clean and stocked with toilet paper, hand soap, and hand towels. A candle is a nice touch in the bathroom as well.

- Make or assemble any food for the party.

- Take care of any final decorating or setup details.

- Buy ice (plan on 1 pound per person) and store it in the freezer and in coolers.

- Chill beverages that will be served cold several hours ahead.

- Empty the dishwasher so it's ready to load after the party.

- Arrange parting gifts/favors by the front door for guests to take on their way out.

a dozen things to remember when hosting a party

1. Plan ahead and make lists.

2. Do as much ahead of time as you can.

3. Don't forget the candles, with only unscented candles at the dinner or buffet table.

4. Use low vases and centerpieces so you don't block the view. No one likes to look over or around an obstacle all night no matter how pretty it is.

5. Make a playlist. I like to have music playing when guests arrive. Maybe something more upbeat to start, then slower music for dinner, at a lower volume (or no music is okay, too). Then crank it back up for after dinner if the mood is right.

6. Set aside time to get ready and tidy up.

7. You will inevitably forget something, so it's nice to have a friend or family member (hubby? daughter who can drive?) on call to run errands if need be. Get them a small gift card to show your appreciation.

8. Make sure you have enough serving plates, bowls, glasses, utensils, etc. Label what goes in each dish and do it ahead of time.

9. Put away any valuables or sentimental breakables.

10. You might want to clean out your bathroom drawers or cabinets if there's anything you don't want people to see. People snoop!

11. Take pictures! They are lovely to look at later.

12. Relax, go with the flow, and *have fun!*

PARTING WORDS

I, for one, like to clean up the next morning. It lets me relive the night and remember how much fun everyone had. Do try to load the dishwasher, put the pots and pans in the sink to soak, and wrap and put away any leftovers before you go to bed. You'll thank me in the morning!

Have a cab company's number (or a car-hailing app like Uber) handy in case a guest overindulges. It's your responsibility to keep your guests safe. If you know someone who likes to get their party on, encourage them to Uber or cab it—or be prepared to let them sleep it off in your guest room.

Make notes the next day about your party. What went well and what might need tweaking for next time? What food was a hit? What decor got positive comments? Did you run out of anything important (drinks, ice)? Keep a notebook that you can refer to so that you remember what was served and who was there. These party notebooks are fun to look back through over the years, too.

Enjoying one of my earliest favorite foods—toast!

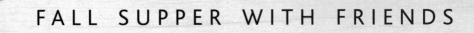

FALL SUPPER WITH FRIENDS

Menu

MAPLE OLD-FASHIONEDS

SMOKED PAPRIKA ALMONDS

GOAT CHEESE AND HONEY CROSTINI

AUTUMN CHOPPED SALAD

BRINED-AND-BRAISED SHORT RIBS

CLASSIC MASHED POTATOES

OVEN-ROASTED VEGETABLES

GINGERSNAP-PUMPKIN CHEESECAKE

Serves 6

Fall is my favorite time of year. I love the crisp air, the smell of falling leaves, getting out my favorite sweatshirt, and sitting by the fire. It's just an invigorating feeling—not too cold yet, but a welcome relief from the heat and humidity of our Tennessee summers. Autumn brings back so many memories of growing up in my hometown (Sharon, Kansas, pop. 200). The season was all about going back to school, football, homecoming, bonfires, and community. In Sharon, we had what we called "soup and chili suppers" where the ladies from the church would make big pots of homemade chili, beef stew, and ham and beans, and serve them with rolls and cornbread on the side. And—oh my goodness—the best cinnamon rolls you have ever tasted!

Community soup and chili suppers were a time to get together, visit, and share a great home-cooked meal. I guess that's one reason fall just feels like the right time to reconnect with friends and family and get cozy with some comfort food! It's also the time of year my girls return to school and we settle back into a routine at home, which I always welcome after the long, lazy days of summer. Family meals become more consistent than in summer, when the girls spend more time out with friends. Fall signals the start of a different kind of cooking at our house, too. We leave behind grilling and fresh summer vegetables for long-simmered braises and slow cooking in the oven. When sweater weather hits, our bodies crave warmth, so it's time for comfort foods like pot roasts, soups, and stews—exactly the sort of dishes it feels good to share. When I cook this meal, it feels like I'm taking really good care of people.

Make this menu for a group of friends or let it become your weekly fall Sunday supper for family. The goal is to slow down and reconnect. To keep the conversation intimate and the atmosphere cozy and relaxed, I like to invite just one or two other couples at most. A small gathering means lots of face-to-face time, so I include people I've really missed and enjoy and who mesh well together. This is also a wonderful opportunity to bring together friends you've wanted to introduce for some time.

If you want to simplify, just pare down the menu and serve a simmering pot of your favorite soup or stew with the Autumn Chopped Salad (page 39) and a big basket of crusty bread or Cornbread with Green Chilies and Pepper Jack Cheese (page 125). Go for it!

my fall supper playlist

1. "Fire and Rain" (James Taylor)

2. "Isn't She Lovely" (Stevie Wonder)

3. "Don't Know Why" (Norah Jones)

4. "1000 Times" (Sara Bareilles)

5. "Just The Way You Are" (Bruno Mars)

6. "Hey There Delilah" (Plain White T's)

7. "100 Years" (Five For Fighting)

8. "High Flying Bird" (Elton John)

9. "Next to Me" (Emeli Sande)

10. "Walking in Memphis" (Marc Cohn)

RUSTIC TEXTURE + FALL COLORS + ORGANIC ELEMENTS

When I think of fall, I think of the colors of the changing leaves: yellow, rust, and dark green. But for this dinner party I used an unexpected twist when it came to the color palette. When I saw how pretty the leafy green plant on my wooden table looked against my cream walls, I decided on a more neutral color scheme with pops of green. (See, I really do get my inspiration from just about anywhere!) So take a cue from my woodsy palette, or choose one of your own, and then layer the shades into your table setting.

I always like to use cream or white plates. Invest in a few good sets of these dishes because they work with any decor (you can find great inexpensive ones at Crate & Barrel—I love me some Crate & Barrel). Arrange the plates on beige place mats or rattan chargers set right on top of the dinner table. I use cream napkins, translucent green water glasses, and a low vase (use two smaller ones if you have a long table) of orange roses to pick up the orange carrots in the roasted veggies.

Small white and dark-green pumpkins from the grocery store look nice in clusters on either side of the vase of roses. It's amazing the array of pumpkins you can find at the grocery store or farmers' market this time of year—white, pale blue, and gray are my favorite choices for this tablescape.

If you are including menu cards on the table, again incorporate your color scheme. Orange or metallic gold type on crisp cream card stock looks nice. You could also buy a few yards of inexpensive white or cream fabric and cut it into menu-sized pieces. Frayed edges are fine and actually add to the overall effect, as do imperfections and wrinkles. Write the menu with fabric pen right on the fabric. Test a small portion first to see if the ink bleeds. If it does, spray the fabric with starch and let it dry before proceeding. This sort of menu is meant to be a keepsake, so if you don't have the prettiest handwriting, enlist the help of someone who does. Make sure to buy enough extra fabric so you can practice!

Small white pumpkins become cool place cards when you write your guests' names on them in paint pen. Or you can use colorful leaves to mark where your guests should sit. Be sure to write names on them carefully (they are delicate) with metallic ink.

DIAL IT UP

I love white pumpkins because they can be worked into fall decor long past Halloween. Of course, you can use them just as they are in an arrangement with fall leaves and flowers, but they make stunning luminarias, too. Hollow out small white pumpkins as you would to make a jack-o'-lantern, then use pumpkin or wood carving tools to punch holes or shapes all over. Set a tea light or votive inside, and light them when guests arrive.

"Fall signals the start of a different kind of cooking at our house."

COOKING GAME PLAN

ONE WEEK BEFORE THE PARTY

- Make the Balsamic–Poppy Seed Dressing and store it in the refrigerator.

- Make the Smoked Paprika Almonds; store in an airtight container.

TWO DAYS BEFORE THE PARTY

- Make the brine for the Brined-and-Braised Short Ribs; cool (see Tip, page 43) and refrigerate overnight.

ONE DAY BEFORE THE PARTY

- Make the Classic Mashed Potatoes through Step 3 and store, covered, in the refrigerator.

- Make the Gingersnap-Pumpkin Cheesecake, wrap tightly, and chill overnight.

- Place the short ribs in the chilled brine and return to the refrigerator to brine overnight.

- For the Autumn Chopped Salad, wash and chop the romaine hearts, cook and crumble the bacon, reserving the fat for browning the short ribs; chill. Toast and chop the pecans; cool and store in a resealable bag at room temperature.

- Toast the bread for the Goat Cheese Crostini; cool and store in a resealable bag at room temperature.

MORNING OF THE PARTY

- Complete the Brined-and-Braised Short Ribs, beginning at Step 3, about 5½ hours before the party; keep warm until serving.

- Prep the ingredients for the Oven-Roasted Vegetables.

- Remove the Gingersnap-Pumpkin Cheesecake from the pan. Slice and chill.

- Mix the Maple Old-Fashioneds and chill.

- Chill the white wine, beer, sodas.

ONE HOUR BEFORE THE PARTY

- Cook the Oven-Roasted Vegetables.

- Prepare the Autumn Chopped Salad, undressed, and chill.

- Bake the Classic Mashed Potatoes and keep warm.

JUST BEFORE THE PARTY

- Set out bowls of the Smoked Paprika Almonds.

- Remove the pitcher of Maple Old-Fashioneds from the refrigerator; stir well.

- Garnish the cheesecake slices; let sit at room temperature.

- Shake the Balsamic–Poppy Seed Dressing well just before serving.

- Spread the goat cheese, then garnish the Goat Cheese Crostini and arrange them on a serving platter.

MAPLE OLD-FASHIONEDS

Serves 6

1½ cups bourbon

⅓ cup high-quality maple syrup (preferably Grade A Dark Amber)

¼ cup fresh orange juice

2 teaspoons orange bitters

6 thin orange slices

I am a bourbon fan, and an old-fashioned is one of my favorite cocktails. This feels like a cooler-weather drink to me. It's important to use good-quality bourbon, since it's the star here. I like Woodford Reserve for this sipper. It's very smooth and easy to drink. But feel free to use your favorite.

1. Combine the bourbon, maple syrup, orange juice, and bitters in a large pitcher. Chill until ready to serve.

2. Serve over ice and garnish with an orange slice.

SANITY SAVER

Stains are pains, but they come with the party territory. Don't let them put a damper on your fun. If red wine gets dribbled on your upholstery or carpet, be nonchalant about it and do what the French do: Put a layer of salt over it to keep the stain from setting and to absorb much of it. You can leave it alone at this point then vacuum it up after the party, or pour a little club soda on it and blot (don't rub) the stain with a clean towel.

SMOKED PAPRIKA ALMONDS

Makes 2 cups

2 cups almonds

1 tablespoon extra-virgin olive oil

2 teaspoons packed light brown sugar

1 teaspoon smoked Spanish paprika

¾ teaspoon kosher salt

Freshly ground black pepper

The small dose of Spanish paprika gives these nuts a smoky, fireside flavor that seems perfect for fall. These are addictive!

1. Preheat the oven to 350°F.

2. Mix the almonds, olive oil, brown sugar, paprika, salt, and pepper in a medium-sized bowl. Toss to coat the almonds evenly. Spread the nuts in a single layer on a large baking sheet. Bake 15 to 20 minutes until fragrant and lightly toasted. Cool to room temperature on a paper towel–lined plate to absorb any excess oil.

Tip: Triple this recipe and you'll have enough for the party plus a cup to send home with each couple. These make a sweet favor wrapped in cellophane and tied with a pretty velvet ribbon in an autumn hue.

GOAT CHEESE AND HONEY CROSTINI

Serves 8 to 10

1 cup walnut pieces

1 French baguette, sliced into ½-inch-thick slices

½ cup olive oil

8 to 10 ounces goat cheese

Honey for drizzling

2 tablespoons rosemary, finely chopped

2 tablespoons thyme, finely chopped

1. Preheat the oven to 350°F.

2. To toast nuts: spread them in a single layer on a baking sheet and bake in the oven for about 10 minutes, or until fragrant and golden, shaking the pan halfway through.

3. Place bread slices on 2 rimmed baking sheets and brush with olive oil. Toast 12 to 15 minutes until crispy but not hard. (Don't burn!) Let cool.

4. Spread each crostino with the goat cheese, sprinkle with the toasted walnuts, and drizzle with the honey. Sprinkle with a bit of the rosemary and thyme.

AUTUMN CHOPPED SALAD

Serves 6

3 romaine hearts, chopped (about 8 cups)

2 small Red Bartlett pears, chopped

¾ cup dried cherries, roughly chopped

¾ cup pecans, chopped and toasted

6 slices thick-cut bacon, cooked and crumbled

½ cup crumbled feta cheese

½ cup fresh flat-leaf parsley leaves

Balsamic–Poppy Seed Dressing

The Balsamic–Poppy Seed Dressing (recipe follows) has a pleasant tanginess that is a nice change of pace from the usual super sweet poppy seed dressings, plus it balances the sweetness of the dried cherries and pears. I dress the salad very lightly and offer more of the dressing for guests to add at the table if they wish.

Combine the lettuce, pears, cherries, pecans, bacon, feta, and parsley on a large platter or in a large bowl. Serve with the Balsamic–Poppy Seed Dressing.

Tip: Have you ever noticed that when you toss a salad all the good stuff (in this case the fruit, nuts, cheese, and bacon) goes to the bottom of the bowl? I like to toss the chopped lettuce with the dressing and then add the rest of the ingredients on top. It's really pretty that way and it ensures that everyone gets a little of everything on their salad plate. This salad is pretty enough to bring to the table to serve.

BALSAMIC—POPPY SEED DRESSING

Makes 1 cup

2 tablespoons
poppy seeds

⅓ cup sugar

6 tablespoons
balsamic vinegar

1 tablespoon grated
yellow onion

2 tablespoons
chopped garlic

2 teaspoons dry
mustard powder

1 teaspoon
kosher salt

½ teaspoon freshly
ground black pepper

⅔ cup extra-virgin
olive oil

1. Combine the poppy seeds, sugar, balsamic vinegar, onion, garlic, mustard powder, salt, and pepper in a food processor, pulsing 3 times. With the food processor running, gradually add the olive oil through the feed tube, blending until incorporated.

2. Pour the dressing into a screw-top jar and store in the refrigerator. When ready to use, shake to recombine.

BRINED-AND-BRAISED SHORT RIBS

 Serves 6

For the brine:

5 quarts water

2 cups kosher salt

2 cups packed light brown sugar

1 celery stalk, cut into chunks

2 carrots, cut into chunks

1 yellow onion, quartered

6 garlic cloves, peeled and crushed

4 sprigs flat-leaf parsley

One 4-inch rosemary sprig

1 bay leaf

8 black peppercorns

¼ teaspoon crushed red pepper flakes

One of John's favorite foods on the planet is short ribs. Some of the best he's eaten were at a restaurant we love in Napa Valley called Tra Vigne founded by chef Michael Chiarello of NapaStyle fame. This is a slight variation on Michael's recipe.

What I love about serving short ribs is that they are a little more special than pot roast but are still firmly rooted in the comfort food category. I also love that they take a little time and TLC to make—there is the browning of the meat, and the caramelizing of the vegetables, and then the slow braise, which makes my whole house smell amazing. When it's crisp outside, the aroma in my kitchen gives an added pleasure to being indoors and makes me a pretty happy girl. These short ribs are a crowd-pleaser served alongside (or on top of . . . up to you) a bed of the most amazing Classic Mashed Potatoes (page 44) you'll taste. This one's a real winner!

1. In a large stockpot, add the water, salt, brown sugar, celery, carrots, onion, garlic, parsley, rosemary, bay leaf, peppercorns, and pepper flakes and bring to a boil, stirring to dissolve the sugar. Allow the brine to cool completely.

2. Add the short ribs to the cooled brine, cover, and refrigerate overnight.

8 pounds bone-in
beef short ribs, cut
into 3-inch pieces

6 slices thick-cut
bacon

2½ cups chopped
yellow onion

1 cup chopped carrots

1 cup chopped celery

1½ tablespoons
unsalted butter

2 cups red wine

6 cups beef stock

Chopped flat-leaf
parsley for garnish

3. Remove the short ribs from the brine and pat dry. Discard the brine.

4. Preheat the oven to 300°F. Heat a large straight-sided sauté pan over medium-high heat. Add the bacon and cook until crispy, then transfer it to a paper towel–lined plate to drain and reserve for another use. Pour the rendered bacon fat into a bowl, leaving 2 tablespoons in the pan. Brown the ribs, in batches, on all sides, adding more rendered bacon fat by the tablespoon as needed. Transfer the browned short ribs to a large roasting pan.

5. Add the onion, carrots, celery, and butter to the sauté pan and cook over medium-high heat until caramelized, 12 to 14 minutes; then spoon the mixture over the short ribs.

6. Pour the red wine into the sauté pan and reduce by half, stirring frequently. Add the beef stock and bring to a boil. Pour the liquid over the short ribs and cover the roasting pan tightly with foil.

7. Bake for 4 hours, or until the meat is fork-tender. Remove the ribs from the oven and let them stand for 20 minutes. To serve, sprinkle with chopped fresh parsley on or beside a bed of Classic Mashed Potatoes (page 44).

Tip: It's really important to cool hot liquids before you refrigerate them or you risk raising the temperature inside your refrigerator and that's not good for perishables. A great trick is to freeze a disposable (BPA-free) plastic water bottle that is three-fourths full and use it to stir the hot liquid to cool it rapidly. Simply wash the exterior of the bottle with soapy water and refreeze to use again.

CLASSIC MASHED POTATOES

Serves 6

1½ pounds russet
potatoes, peeled
and cut into
2-inch chunks

1¼ teaspoons kosher
salt, or to taste

¼ cup (½ stick)
salted butter, cut into
pieces, softened

4 ounces cream
cheese, softened

¾ cup finely
shredded Parmigiano-
Reggiano

½ cup sour cream

¼ to ½ cup milk,
warmed

¾ teaspoon chopped
fresh thyme

¼ teaspoon freshly
ground black pepper

Pinch of nutmeg

Paprika, optional

½ teaspoon chopped
fresh chives

This is my go-to recipe for fluffy, flavorful mashed potatoes.

1. Preheat the oven to 350°F. Add the potatoes to a large saucepan and cover with cold water by at least 1 inch. Add 1 teaspoon of the salt and bring to a boil. Reduce the heat to medium and cook, partially covered, until the potatoes are very tender, 12 to 15 minutes. Drain and return the potatoes to the pan.

2. Break up the potatoes with a potato masher or a handheld mixer on low speed. Gradually add 3 tablespoons of the butter and beat until incorporated. Gradually add the cream cheese, Parmigiano-Reggiano, and sour cream, beating well after each addition. Gradually add the warm milk, 2 tablespoons at a time, until incorporated and the potatoes are fluffy and light. (You may not need all the milk.) Stir in the thyme and remaining ¼ teaspoon salt, or more to taste, the pepper, and the nutmeg.

3. Butter an 8 × 8-inch baking dish. Spoon the potatoes into the dish, smoothing the top. Use a small spatula or fork to create peaks on the surface to aid browning.

4. Sprinkle the top with the paprika, if desired. Cut the remaining tablespoon of butter into small pieces and sprinkle them over the potatoes. Bake 30 minutes, or until lightly browned. Sprinkle with chives and serve warm. (If baking the potatoes directly from the refrigerator, increase bake time to 1 hour.)

OVEN-ROASTED VEGETABLES

Serves 6

12 baby carrots with tops, peeled and trimmed

12 baby zucchini

1 pound Campari tomatoes on the vine

1 garlic bulb, cloves separated, peeled, and smashed

3 tablespoons extra-virgin olive oil

2 tablespoons fresh rosemary, finely chopped

2 teaspoons kosher salt

1 teaspoon freshly ground black pepper

¼ cup freshly grated Parmigiano-Reggiano

I just recently learned how to roast vegetables. When I was growing up, boiling everything was the norm. And then came steaming, which I still love! But roasting vegetables in the oven brings out a deeper, richer flavor that just goes really nicely with the beef and potatoes. Feel free to substitute fresh green beans, Brussels sprouts, new potatoes, or any other vegetable. These roasted veggies add a beautiful pop of color to the plate. I like to include a few short sprigs of rosemary in the mix for interest in addition to the chopped rosemary.

1. Preheat the oven to 350°F.

2. Place the carrots, zucchini, tomatoes, and garlic in a large bowl. Drizzle with the olive oil and sprinkle with the rosemary, salt, and pepper, tossing to coat. Transfer the vegetables to a large rimmed baking sheet.

3. Bake for 40 to 45 minutes, stirring once after 25 minutes until the vegetables are tender and browned. Spoon the vegetables into a platter and top with the cheese to serve.

GINGERSNAP-PUMPKIN CHEESECAKE

Serves 10 to 12

2 cups crushed
gingersnap cookies
(30 to 40 cookies),
plus extra for garnish

¼ cup packed light
brown sugar

6 tablespoons
unsalted butter,
melted

3 8-ounce packages
of cream cheese,
softened

1 cup granulated
sugar

1 teaspoon ground
cinnamon

½ teaspoon ground
allspice

½ teaspoon ground
ginger

¼ teaspoon ground
nutmeg

3 large eggs

This makes a nine-inch cheesecake and it is very rich on top of an already rich meal, so slice it thinly, knowing that you will have about half the cheesecake left over. Wrap the remaining cheesecake tightly and refrigerate to enjoy another night.

1. Prepare a 9-inch springform pan by tracing it onto a sheet of parchment paper. Lightly grease the bottom of the pan. Cut out the round of parchment and place it in the greased pan and then lightly grease the paper (a little trick I learned from Martha).

2. Preheat the oven to 350°F. Place the crushed gingersnaps and brown sugar in a food processor and process until finely chopped. Add the melted butter and process until thoroughly combined. Press the mixture into the bottom and up the sides of the springform pan. Chill for 10 to 20 minutes.

3. Beat the cream cheese and granulated sugar in a medium bowl with an electric mixer until light and fluffy. Add the cinnamon, allspice, ginger, and nutmeg and mix until combined. Add the eggs, one at a time, mixing just until the yolk disappears. Add the cream, vanilla, and pumpkin puree, mixing to just combine.

2 tablespoons heavy cream

2 teaspoons vanilla extract

1 15-ounce can pure pumpkin puree (not pumpkin pie filling)

1 cup heavy cream, whipped, or Chantilly cream (see Note), optional

Crushed toffee bar, such as Heath, optional

4. Remove the crust from the refrigerator. Pour the cheesecake batter into the prepared crust. Bake 1 hour and 15 minutes, or until the center is almost set. Run a sharp knife around the edge of the cheesecake to help prevent it from cracking as it cools. Let the cheesecake cool at least 30 minutes. Cover and chill in the refrigerator overnight.

5. To serve, remove the cheesecake from the pan and transfer it to a serving plate. Slice into 10 to 12 wedges and top each with a dollop of whipped cream and a sprinkle of crushed gingersnaps or finely crushed toffee bar.

Tip: If you don't have all the spices on hand and must go to the store, purchase a single jar of pumpkin pie spice and use 2¼ teaspoons in place of the ground spices called for here.

Note: To make 2 cups of Chantilly cream, whip 1 cup of cold heavy cream with 1 tablespoon of confectioners' sugar and ½ teaspoon of vanilla extract.

BOUNTIFUL TUSCAN FEAST

Menu

CAMPARI SPRITZ

ANTIPASTI PLATTER

PROSCIUTTO-WRAPPED MELON

ZUCCHINI FRITTATA

PANZANELLA

HUNTER'S CHICKEN

PEPERONATA

GREEN BEANS WITH LEMON

CREAMY POLENTA

EGGPLANT PARMESAN

BUTTERNUT RAVIOLI

TIRAMISU

Serves 8 to 10

What I love most about Italian food is its simplicity. You typically use only a few ingredients, and the end result comes out delicious and comforting. When a recipe calls for only a select number of ingredients, it's important to use the best-quality, freshest ones you can find. You can really taste the difference when you do. I rely on my local farmers' market and my butcher to help me.

This particular menu comes from two Italian friends from Tuscany, George Valentino Pestritu and his wife, Larisa Laudat. They visited us for a week in Nashville and cooked for our family every night! A few pounds later, I asked if they would create an authentic Tuscan menu, with recipes, for my book and they agreed. What they cooked up is a casual, family-style menu designed with the idea of everyone passing platters of food at the table. The meal is abundant, so serve small portions of each dish to ensure that your guests get to taste a bit of everything without feeling stuffed. And feel free to pare the recipes down to suit your tastes and crowd. Valentino suggests picking just one side dish to go with the chicken if the menu feels overwhelming—the Peperonata, Creamy Polenta, or Green Beans with Lemon. Always adapt the menu offerings in this book to suit your time and temperament in the kitchen! This gathering is meant to be informal and relaxed, so play around with the recipes and pick and choose your favorites.

It's worth noting that Italians take their time and really make a meal last, sometimes over several hours. This is an idea I can appreciate, as a busy mom always pulled in a million directions. When I'm home from a tour, it is so relaxing to sit for a long evening around the table with friends in an inviting environment. Linger over your plates and keep the wine and conversation flowing. There is nothing better than sharing laughter and love over food, and this Tuscan menu truly sets the scene for a warm and special evening. Thank you, Valentino and Larisa!

This menu is exactly what Valentino and Larisa served up when they were visiting. I wanted you to enjoy all of their creations, but I would recommend you scale this feast down to suit your guests.

my tuscan party playlist

1. "That's Amore" (Dean Martin)

2. "La vie en rose" (Edith Piaf) (I know, I know, it's French)

3. "Volare" (Bobby Rydell)

4. "We Speak No Americano" (Yolanda Be Cool & DCUP)

5. "Something Stupid" (the Mavericks)

6. "Buona Sera" (Dean Martin)

7. "Que Sera, Sera" (Doris Day)

8. "Attenti al lupo" (Lucio Dalla)

9. "O Sole Mio" (Frank Patterson or Il Volo)

10. "Follia d'amore" (Raphael Gualazzi)

NATURAL ELEMENTS + TUSCAN PALETTE + CLASSIC ITALIAN FOOD

When setting the mood for a Tuscan feast, think relaxed and warm. I like to stick to varied shades of yellow, orange, cream, and touches of green, all colors that remind me of the hills of Tuscany—and are perfect for autumn, too. To keep the decor natural and simple, I head out to my garden to collect some clippings, and at the grocery store I gather up fresh flowers and fruit. Bunches of herbs, a few lemons, and artichokes add Old World flair. And sunflowers say Italy to me, so I like to arrange them in low vases for the table. Add a few bowls of pomegranates for an extra pop of color.

If you have an old wooden harvest table, don't even bother with a tablecloth. If not, consider a burlap tablecloth. Burlap is a great inexpensive fabric that adds texture and rustic character. Either make one yourself by cutting yardage of inexpensive burlap with shears (the edges will fray a bit over time) or invest in having a few made with more finished edges to fit your table perfectly. I use my burlap tablecloths all the time. But if you don't have one, don't sweat it. A crisp white linen tablecloth works just fine, too. Choose basic white or solid-colored napkins or look for ones that have a pattern that feels Italian or just suits your decor.

As a finishing touch, I place a sprig of fresh rosemary from my garden on top of each napkin—pretty and simple. If I'm using a printed menu, I place the menu on top

of the napkin and lay the rosemary beside it or tuck it into the top of the napkin or the napkin ring. Just play around and do what looks prettiest to you. Rosemary, basil, parsley, and other potted herbs are fragrant centerpieces that your guests can take home at the end of the night.

DIAL IT UP

Make a lasting memento for guests by using small potted herbs at each place setting. Simply wrap the plastic nursery pot with burlap secured with twine and accent it with a handwritten recipe card from the evening's menu or a plant marker for the garden.

Sunflowers say "Italy" to me.

COOKING GAME PLAN

THREE DAYS BEFORE THE PARTY

- Chill the Prosecco, club soda, and white wine.

- Make the Tomato Sauce for the Eggplant Parmesan; cool and refrigerate.

- Slice oranges to use as cocktail garnishes. Place them in a resealable plastic bag and refrigerate until needed.

TWO DAYS BEFORE THE PARTY

- Slice the zucchini and chop the onions for the Frittata. Place in separate resealable plastic bags and refrigerate.

- Chop the peppers for the Peperonata, store in a resealable plastic bag, and refrigerate.

- Trim and blanch the green beans for the Green Beans with Lemon. Drain well and dry on paper towels, then transfer to a resealable plastic bag and refrigerate.

THE DAY BEFORE THE PARTY

- Leave a fresh loaf of Tuscan-style bread unwrapped on the counter overnight for the Panzanella.

- Peel and slice the cucumbers and place them in a resealable plastic bag and refrigerate for the Panzanella.

- Marinate the chicken for the Hunter's Chicken.

- Make the fettunta and pumpkin bread, if including, for the Antipasti Platter. Wrap and store at room temperature.

THE MORNING OF THE PARTY

- Arrange the meats, cheese, and fruits for the Antipasti Platter, cover, and chill until serving.

- Prepare the Tiramisu and refrigerate until serving.

- Dice the tomatoes, reserving the juices, for the Panzanella.

THREE HOURS BEFORE THE PARTY

- Slice the eggplant and let it stand as in Step 1 of the recipe for Eggplant Parmesan.

- Drain the chicken, and let it come to room temperature for 30 minutes before flouring and browning it.

TWO HOURS BEFORE THE PARTY

- Prepare the Prosciutto-Wrapped Melon; chill until serving.

- Prepare the Peperonata; keep it warm until serving.

- Place the roasting pan(s) with the Hunter's Chicken in the oven to finish.

- Complete Step 2 of the Eggplant Parmesan recipe.

ONE HOUR BEFORE THE PARTY

- Prepare the Panzanella up to Step 4.

- Prepare the Frittata; keep warm until serving.

- Complete the Eggplant Parmesan.

THIRTY MINUTES BEFORE THE PARTY

- Prepare the Green Beans with Lemon.

- Complete the Panzanella.

- Prepare the Creamy Polenta and keep warm, thinning with hot water as needed to serve.

- Prepare the Butternut Ravioli with Sage Leaves.

- Arrange fettunta and pumpkin bread slices, if using, for the Antipasti Platter.

- Mix a pitcher of the Campari Spritz minus the ice for self-service, or set out chilled bottles and ice for making drinks to order.

CAMPARI SPRITZ

Makes 1 cocktail

Prosecco

Campari

Club soda

Orange juice

Orange slices for garnish

Larisa's recipe can be used to make individual cocktails or to whip up a big batch for a self-serve station. If you're making this in bulk, don't add the ice or it will dilute the drink as it melts. Just have a bucket of ice nearby for filling the glasses.

Mix 2 parts Prosecco with 1 part Campari in an ice-filled cocktail glass. Add a splash of club soda and a splash of orange juice. Drop a thin slice of orange into the drink to serve.

If you're not familiar with it, Campari is a vivid red *amaro*, or Italian digestive bitters, made from herbs and botanicals mixed with alcohol and sugar. It has a bittersweet orange flavor. It was originally created as a medicinal that people sipped to ease an upset stomach, but it has become a popular cocktail mixer.

ANTIPASTI 101

- Stick to just a few varieties each of meat and cheese.

- Make it interesting. Choose a sampling of items from a particular region or vary the flavors and textures by including a fresh mild cheese, a dry aged cheese, and a stronger-flavored ripened cheese.

- Include fruit or pickled and brined items as a palate cleanser.

- Label the meats and cheeses if you wish.

- Replenish the bread and crackers often.

ANTIPASTI PLATTER

Meats (pick 2 or 3): 6
ounces of each, thinly
sliced

Bresaola

Prosciutto di Parma

Soppressata

Tuscan salami

Cheeses (pick 2 or 3):
1 pound of each, cut or
crumbled

Gorgonzola Piccante

Mozzarella di bufala

Parmigiano-Reggiano
drizzled with aged
balsamic vinegar

Pecorino Toscano

Stracchino

Add-ons (pick a few):

Fettunta: 1 loaf sliced
and toasted Italian bread
rubbed with garlic, plus
olive oil for dipping

1 large bunch or
2 small bunches red
seedless grapes

½ cup honey for drizzling

2 cups pecans

1 loaf sliced pumpkin
bread

2 thinly sliced pears

Meat and cheese plates are pretty common cocktail-hour fare, so put an interesting spin on the usual setup here by seeking out authentic Tuscan meats and cheeses for guests to sample. Make friends with the guy behind the counter at your local cheese shop. He can lead the way and help you make some great selections. Label them with little flags or arrange them on a piece of slate with the name of each item written in chalk. An assortment of cold cuts and cheeses from your local grocery store is absolutely fine here, too, but it's always fun to try new things and share them with your guests. Valentino and Larisa served a platter of thinly sliced pears, grapes, and pumpkin bread (as unusual as that sounds!) along with four different cheeses, arranged from mildest to strongest: mozzarella di bufala, stracchino, Pecorino Toscano, and Gorgonzola Piccante. Larisa drizzled honey over the first two cheeses and topped pieces of pumpkin bread with a pear slice, Gorgonzola crumbles, and a walnut. It was unexpected and so delicious!

PROSCIUTTO-WRAPPED MELON

1 large ripe cantaloupe, seeded and sliced

3 ounces thinly sliced prosciutto di Parma

Freshly ground black pepper

This classic Italian appetizer is super simple to make. Cut the flesh of 1 ripe cantaloupe into ½-inch wedges and wrap each with a ½-inch-wide "belt" of prosciutto made by cutting prosciutto slices lengthwise into thirds. Arrange on a platter and season with freshly cracked black pepper to serve.

ZUCCHINI FRITTATA

Serves 8 to 10

3 tablespoons extra-
virgin olive oil

1 small yellow onion,
chopped

6 to 8 small zucchini,
chopped (about
6 cups)

10 large eggs

1 cup chopped flat-
leaf parsley

1 cup freshly grated
Parmigiano-Reggiano

1 teaspoon
kosher salt

½ teaspoon freshly
ground black pepper

*This Italian omelet is rich and delicious. Though this meal is
served family-style, it helps to control portion sizes, so slice
the frittata into skinny wedges before passing at the table. You
want your guests to sample and savor everything, but not be so
stuffed that they'll roll out the door!*

1. Position an oven rack in the center and preheat the oven to 350°F.

2. Heat the oil in a 12-inch ovenproof nonstick or well-seasoned
cast-iron skillet over low heat. Add the onion and sauté 5 minutes,
then add the zucchini to sweat, gently stirring until softened but not
browned, 8 to 10 minutes.

3. Meanwhile, whisk together the eggs, parsley, cheese, salt,
and the pepper until thoroughly combined. Pour the egg mixture over
the zucchini and stir once to distribute the zucchini evenly. Increase
the heat to medium-low and cook 5 minutes without stirring, until the
edges have pulled away from the sides of the skillet. Transfer the
skillet to the oven and bake for 8 to 10 minutes, or until the center
is just set. Run a spatula around the edge of the pan, then slide the
frittata onto a serving plate and slice it into wedges. Serve warm.

*Tip: It is extremely important (in my opinion) to have an ovenproof
nonstick skillet for this recipe. It's so satisfying when the whole thing
slides beautifully onto the plate. Not so much when it doesn't.*

PANZANELLA

Serves 8 to 10

1 medium red onion,
halved and thinly sliced

½ cup plus 4 to 5
teaspoons red wine
vinegar

10 slices of day-old
Tuscan-style bread,
cut into 1-inch cubes
(about 10 cups)

8 large ripe heirloom
tomatoes

2 medium cucumbers,
peeled, halved
lengthwise, and sliced

1 cup chopped fresh
basil, plus more for
garnish

1 cup extra-virgin olive
oil

2 teaspoons kosher salt

1 teaspoon freshly
ground black pepper

Parmigiano-Reggiano
for garnish

I could eat this bread salad every day! It's best when tomatoes are at their prime in late summer, which is when I like to host this party. Leave a fresh loaf of Tuscan-style bread, unwrapped, on the counter overnight for the best texture.

1. Preheat the oven to 350°F. Combine the red onion and the ½ cup of red wine vinegar in a small bowl and let stand for at least 15 minutes, stirring occasionally.

2. Meanwhile, spread the bread cubes in a single layer on a sheet pan (or two pans, if needed) and bake for 12 to 14 minutes, or until golden and crunchy. Remove from the oven and let cool.

3. Dice the tomatoes and place them in a large serving bowl, adding the juices as well. Drain the red onion and discard the vinegar. Add the marinated onion to the tomatoes along with the cucumber and basil. Add the olive oil, the remaining 4 to 5 teaspoons of red wine vinegar, salt, and pepper and set the salad aside to let the flavors come together, 30 minutes.

4. Add the toasted bread to the tomato mixture. Sprinkle with the salt and pepper and toss to combine. Let stand for 20 minutes before serving. Garnish with shaved Parmigiano-Reggiano and a few tiny or torn basil leaves.

Tip: Too much longer than 20 minutes gives you a soggy salad. So time accordingly.

HUNTER'S CHICKEN

Serves 8 to 10

2 whole (4- to 5-pound) farm-raised chickens, cut into serving pieces

Kosher salt

Freshly ground black pepper

3 garlic cloves

7 to 8 fresh sage leaves

½ bottle dry white wine, plus ¾ cup

Flour for dusting

½ cup extra-virgin olive oil

¼ teaspoon crushed red pepper flakes

2 14½-ounce cans diced tomatoes (preferably San Marzano), drained

1 cup whole pitted Kalamata or Taggiasca olives

2 cups fresh sliced baby portobello mushrooms

2 cups chicken stock

This is a savory, rustic, satisfying main course dish. Feel free to use all breast pieces if that's what your family prefers. Just make sure they are skin-on, bone-in breasts. If you have a Dutch oven or roasting pan, you can prep this from start to finish all in the same pan. Just place the roasting pan over two burners.

1. Rinse the chicken and pat it dry, then season liberally with salt and pepper. Place the pieces in a large bowl. Smash and peel the garlic and add it to the bowl with the sage leaves and the half bottle of wine, turning the pieces to coat. Marinate in the refrigerator, turning the pieces occasionally, at least 4 hours but preferably overnight.

2. Preheat the oven to 350°F. Drain the chicken, discarding the marinade. Dust the chicken pieces lightly with the flour. Heat a Dutch oven or 16 x 13-inch roasting pan over medium-high heat for 1 minute, then add the oil. When the oil shimmers, add the red pepper flakes and stir about 1 minute.

3. Working in batches, brown 3 to 4 pieces of chicken at a time, skin side down, 5 minutes per side until the skin is golden brown, and set aside.

4. Add the remaining ¾ cup wine to the pan, stirring to loosen any browned bits, and boil for 5 minutes, or until reduced by half. Stir in the tomatoes, olives, mushrooms, and chicken stock to blend. Return the chicken to the pan and spoon the tomato mixture

over the chicken. Cover the roasting pan tightly with aluminum foil, or if using a Dutch oven, cover with the lid.

5. Bake for 45 minutes, then uncover and cook for an additional 20 minutes, or until the juices run clear when the chicken is pierced between the leg and the thigh with the tip of a knife. Serve with pan juices over Creamy Polenta (page 73) with a side of Peperonata (page 71).

PEPERONATA

Serves 8 to 10

Made by braising sweet peppers with herbs and garlic, this sauce is a great garnish for meats of any kind and is often stirred into hot pasta or layered in sandwiches.

¼ cup extra-virgin olive oil

6 garlic cloves, peeled

2 tablespoons chopped fresh rosemary

3 large red bell peppers, coarsely chopped

3 large green bell peppers, coarsely chopped

3 large yellow bell peppers, coarsely chopped

1 teaspoon kosher salt

½ teaspoon freshly ground black pepper

Preheat the oven to 350°F. Heat the oil in a large sauté pan over medium heat. Add the garlic cloves and rosemary and cook 1 minute until fragrant. Add the bell peppers, salt, and pepper. Increase the heat to high and cook for 15 minutes, stirring often, until tender. Transfer the pepper mixture to an ovenproof dish and bake for 20 minutes in the oven until the peppers are meltingly tender.

GREEN BEANS WITH LEMON

Serves 8 to 10

2 pounds fresh green
beans, trimmed

¼ cup extra-virgin
olive oil

Finely grated zest of
1 small lemon

3 garlic cloves,
thinly sliced

1 teaspoon sea salt

I love how fresh and vibrant these beans are with just a hint of citrus. To get a jump start on the menu, I blanch and shock the beans ahead of time.

1. Fill a large bowl with ice water. Bring a large pot of generously salted water to a boil. Add the green beans and let the water return to a boil. Cook 2 to 4 minutes, depending on thickness, until the beans are bright green and crisp-tender. Drain and plunge the beans into the ice water to shock, or stop the cooking.

2. Add the olive oil and lemon zest to a pot over low heat and warm for 3 minutes. Add the garlic and cook over medium-low heat until it begins to soften and turn golden, about 30 seconds. (Be careful not to burn!) Quickly add the beans to the pot and toss to coat with the infused oil. Transfer the green beans to a platter and sprinkle with the sea salt.

CREAMY POLENTA

Serves 8 to 10

8 cups water

1½ teaspoons kosher salt

2 cups coarse polenta (not quick-cooking)

3 tablespoons unsalted butter

Consider polenta to be the grits or mashed potatoes of Italy. I use it as a comforting base for braised or stewed dishes, plus it's supereasy to prepare (if you don't mind all that stirring!). You really can't mess it up, either. If it gets too thick, simply stir in hot water, a quarter cup at a time, until the mixture is the consistency you're after.

Bring the water to a boil in a large saucepan. Add the salt, then stir in the polenta. Cook over medium heat, stirring often, until it starts to thicken; reduce the heat to low. Be careful—polenta often splatters at this point. Continue to stir until the polenta has cooked for 30 minutes, then remove from the heat. Add the butter and let it melt to create a film on top of the polenta, which keeps it from getting dry. Cover the pan and hold at this point until serving time. Stir in the melted butter; taste and adjust seasoning to serve.

Toasted or grilled polenta is a great base for appetizers. Simply spread the Creamy Polenta in a lightly greased glass 9 × 13-inch baking dish, cover, and chill overnight until set. Turn the polenta over on a cutting board and slice into small rectangles or triangles. Grill these on both sides in a hot grill pan or on a grill until grill marks appear, about 10 minutes. Top with whatever you like. A spoonful of Peperonata and some crumbled goat cheese are delicious toppers!

EGGPLANT PARMESAN

Serves 8 to 10

3 medium eggplants,
sliced into ¼-inch
rounds

1 tablespoon
kosher salt

3 tablespoons extra-
virgin olive oil

½ teaspoon freshly
ground black pepper

5 cups Tomato Sauce
(recipe follows)

32 ounces fresh
mozzarella (di bufala
or fior di latte), cut
into ¼-inch slices

10 ounces freshly
shaved Parmigiano-
Reggiano

It's really important to salt and drain the eggplant before you make this recipe. Skip that step and the resulting dish can be soggy (trust me . . . I know!). Baking the slices before layering them in the dish browns them a bit and dries them out further so that they can really absorb the flavorful sauce. Buy quality fresh mozzarella for this dish.

1. Preheat the oven to 400°F.

2. Place the eggplant slices on baking sheets and sprinkle both sides evenly with the salt. Transfer to a colander set over a bowl and drain, 45 minutes to 1 hour. Wipe the salt and any remaining moisture from the slices with paper towels.

3. Place the eggplant slices on parchment-lined baking sheets and drizzle them evenly with the olive oil, then sprinkle with the pepper. Bake for 20 minutes, or until lightly browned.

4. Spoon 1 cup of tomato sauce into a 13 × 9-inch baking dish. Layer one-third of the eggplant slices over the tomato sauce, slightly overlapping the slices. Spoon 1¼ cups of tomato sauce over the eggplant. Layer one-third of the mozzarella slices over the tomato sauce and sprinkle with one-third of the shaved Parmigiano-Reggiano. Repeat twice.

5. Place the baking dish in the oven and reduce the temperature to 350°F. Bake 45 to 50 minutes, or until golden brown.

TOMATO SAUCE

Makes a generous 7 cups

3 tablespoons extra-virgin olive oil

1 large red onion, chopped

¼ teaspoon crushed red pepper flakes

4 garlic cloves, pressed

3 28-ounce cans whole peeled tomatoes, preferably San Marzano

1 cup water

1 tablespoon kosher salt

½ teaspoon freshly ground black pepper

1 cup chopped fresh basil

1 teaspoon chopped fresh oregano

1. Pour the tomatoes into a large bowl and crush them into smaller pieces with your hands. Set aside.

2. Heat the olive oil in a large Dutch oven over medium-low heat. Add the onion and crushed red pepper flakes and cook for 8 to 10 minutes, or until the onion is softened, stirring constantly. Add the garlic and stir for 30 seconds, then reduce the heat to low.

3. Add the crushed tomatoes and water to the onion-garlic mixture, stirring to combine. Cook, uncovered, for 1 hour.

4. Season the sauce with the salt and pepper. Stir in the basil and oregano.

BUTTERNUT RAVIOLI

Serves 8 to 10

2 9-ounce packages
of butternut squash
ravioli

½ cup (1 stick)
unsalted butter

¼ cup extra-virgin
olive oil

20 fresh sage leaves

6 tablespoons grated
Parmigiano-Reggiano

2 amaretto biscuits,
crushed (optional)

Kosher salt, to taste

Freshly ground black
pepper, to taste

Using premade or frozen ravioli makes this dish so quick to put together, which is helpful with a menu this large. I love butternut squash, especially with this simple sauce.

1. Cook the butternut squash ravioli per package directions and drain, reserving ½ cup of the cooking water.

2. Melt the butter with the olive oil in a large nonstick pan over medium heat, and add the sage. Add the cooked ravioli and a few tablespoons of the reserved cooking water. Toss to coat the ravioli with the creamy sauce.

3. Transfer the ravioli and sauce to a platter and garnish with the Parmigiano-Reggiano and amaretti, if desired. Season with salt and freshly ground black pepper to taste. Serve 2 or 3 ravioli per person, depending on size.

SANITY SAVER

I'm a firm believer in embellishing prepared foods or store-bought ingredients to make them special yet really take the pressure off party prep. This pasta is a perfect example.

TIRAMISU

 Serves 8 to 10

2 cups strong black
coffee or espresso

1 cup sugar

3 tablespoons
dark rum

40 ladyfingers,
preferably Savoiardi
brand

6 large egg yolks

1 teaspoon vanilla
extract

16 ounces
mascarpone, softened

1 cup heavy cream

½ cup finely shaved
bittersweet chocolate

3 tablespoons
unsweetened cocoa

Tiramisu *literally means "pick-me-up." Not only is it a deliciously decadent dessert, but it comes soaked with espresso to buffer all that sugar and alcohol. Depending on your pan, you may need to trim the ladyfingers to get a uniform fit. While many recipes call for soaking the ladyfingers in the coffee, I find that they easily fall apart. Brushing them lightly with a basting brush gets them wet without oversoaking.*

1. Combine the hot coffee or espresso, ¼ cup of the sugar, and the rum in a small bowl, whisking until the sugar is dissolved.

2. Arrange the ladyfingers in a single layer on a baking sheet and, using a basting brush, brush the tops lightly with the coffee-rum mixture until all are covered. Set the ladyfingers aside to allow the liquid to soak through while you prepare the custard.

3. Mix the egg yolks, the remaining ¾ cup sugar, and the vanilla in a large bowl with an electric hand mixer whisk at medium-high speed for 6 to 8 minutes, until pale and thickened. Reduce the speed to low and add the mascarpone, a spoonful at a time, whisking well after each addition until all is incorporated.

4. Whip the heavy cream in a separate bowl until soft peaks form, then gently fold the whipped cream into the custard mixture to lighten.

$5.$ Arrange a layer of ladyfingers in a 9 × 13-inch baking dish, trimming to fit as needed (you should be able to fit about 20). Spread half the custard over the top. Repeat with another layer of ladyfingers and the remaining custard. Refrigerate at least 4 hours or up to 8 hours. Sprinkle with the shaved chocolate and cocoa before serving.

Note: This recipe calls for raw eggs, so be sure yours are very fresh. Look for pasteurized eggs in the grocery store if you wish. If you don't have enough time to prep this delicious dessert, don't worry! Pick up some Italian pastries at your local bakery. You just cooked a big Italian feast; a store-bought dessert is always an acceptable swap to the menus in my book.

Thanks to Valentino and Larisa for sharing this menu and time around the table with my family.

FAMILY PIZZA NIGHT

Menu

ITALIAN SODAS

BASIC PIZZA DOUGH

MAKE-YOUR-OWN PIZZA

MONDAY NIGHT MARINARA SAUCE

TOSSED SALAD WITH LEMON-PARMESAN DRESSING

PEACHES WITH LEMON SHORTBREAD

Serves 6

John and I believe family dinners are really important. We've always tried our best to eat together at the dinner table several times a week and my girls know it's a priority. I believe that meals at the family table provide an opportunity for kids to share the events of their day, practice basic manners, and learn to listen to each other. I think these shared meals are one of the reasons my girls have become such great conversationalists. They really miss it when our schedules get so busy that we skip more than a few dinners in a row. Shared meals are one of our family traditions that I'm confident the girls will carry on with their own families one day, and that makes me happy! I encourage you to create your own family night of fun and great conversation.

Over the years I have taught the girls to cook and they enjoy helping out in the kitchen. I can always count on one or two of them to set the table and they clear their plates afterward. Lending a hand in the kitchen helps them realize the effort that goes into making a house run smoothly, plus it fosters teamwork, closeness, and a sense of responsibility. They can get pretty creative when it comes to setting the table and creating a vibe. I'll admit, this is my favorite part of entertaining as well, so I guess it rubbed off. I feel proud that I have set an example for them to make the "everyday" special. Whether it's grabbing a bunch of herbs from the garden and putting them in a vase for the table, playing music while we cook, or creating place cards just for fun, they appreciate making the ordinary special. Now, I'm not saying I don't ever eat a sandwich off of a paper towel while standing at the kitchen island, because I often do just that! But making the effort to set a pretty table or create an inviting atmosphere is definitely worth it.

This year Delaney and I made the Christmas breakfast together for the first time, which was so much more fun than being in the kitchen all by myself. Ava has shown an interest in cooking since she was really little, always asking, "Can I do that?" She helps me prepare lasagna and we bake together on occasion. She makes a mean

smoothie, too! Delaney is my baker and is sooo much better at it than I am. Emma would honestly rather have someone cook for her (a diva in training . . . I respect that!), but she happily helps out in other ways and she makes great scrambled eggs!

A few years ago we started "Make-Your-Own Pizza" night at our house. The idea hit me when I saw pizza dough at the grocery store and thought, "How fun would it be to make pizza together at home?" (As I've said, I always try to be open to inspiration, as it can come out of the blue!) I brought home the dough and a bunch of different toppings and we had such a great time together that a new tradition was born.

It's fun to experiment with different topping combinations. In my family we all like pizza sauce and cheese, cheese, and more cheese, but my favorite toppings are garlic, a medley of mozzarella, Parmigiano-Reggiano, and goat cheese, topped with basil, black olives, and jalapeño slices. Sometimes I will even add ham and pineapple to all that! John sticks with a garlic, goat cheese, and pepperoni combo. Delaney layers on all kinds of cheese, pepperoni, garlic, basil, and pineapple, while Emma tops "all the green stuff" with pepperoni and pineapple, too. Ava keeps it simple with a cheesy pizza topped with pepperoni. The great thing about this dinner is that everybody gets to have fun making their food exactly the way they want while we are in the kitchen together.

my pizza night playlist

1. "Count On Me" (Bruno Mars)

2. "One Big Love" (Patty Griffin)

3. "Drops of Jupiter" (Train)

4. "Home" (Johnny Swim)

5. "Rollin' in the Deep" (Adele)

6. "Just Give Me a Reason" (Pink and Nate Reuss)

7. "Breaking the Chains of Love" (Fitz and the Tantrums)

8. "Use Somebody" (Kings of Leon)

9. "Soldier" (Gavin DeGraw)

10. "Where Is the Love" (Black Eyed Peas)

KID CRAFTS + TABLE GAMES + FAMILY-FRIENDLY CASUAL

Even though we usually do this as a family, it is just as fun with friends in the mix. I love a crowd hanging out in the kitchen, drinks in hand, talking and listening to music while assembling pizzas. It's a lively and fun idea for a party that can be as casual or as special as you wish.

Kids, especially the smaller ones, love crafts, so put them to work making place cards that they can decorate any way they like. Shape each card like a slice of pizza and they can draw the toppings they think match each guest. Their artwork adds whimsy to the table and keeps them occupied while the pizzas bake. I love the contrast of a casual, eat-with-your-fingers affair paired with pretty cloth napkins, but a roll of paper towels sitting in the middle of the table works, too. Arrange silverware in glasses on the buffet with plates stacked so people can serve themselves salad and their pizza before taking a seat. Set out small bowls of red pepper flakes and freshly grated Parmigiano-Reggiano on the buffet or the table for guests to sprinkle on their pizza. The pizzas themselves with their bright toppings take center stage, so no need to fuss too much with the decor. This is a roll-up-your-sleeves-and-dig-in kind of party.

SANITY SAVER

Sometimes you need to break the ice! Someone gave us a game called Table Topics. Each person draws a card and reads the question out loud, then we go around the table taking turns answering it. We love this game! It brings up interesting points of conversation and ideas we might not think of otherwise. It's also great for a party with both kids and adults because it encourages interaction and really gets the conversation going. I think it's a fun way for kids to hold court and be heard, and it helps with their conversation skills. For most of us, our lives are so busy that it's important to take this time to connect.

COOKING GAME PLAN

ONE WEEK BEFORE THE PARTY

- Make the Lemon Shortbread dough, roll, wrap, and freeze.

- Make the Basic Pizza Dough, divide into portions, and freeze individually in resealable freezer bags.

TWO DAYS BEFORE THE PARTY

- Remove the Lemon Shortbread dough from freezer; let stand 30 minutes. Slice, bake, cool, and transfer to an airtight container.

ONE DAY BEFORE THE PARTY

- Make the Monday Night Marinara Sauce.

- Transfer pizza dough from freezer to refrigerator to thaw.

MORNING OF THE PARTY

- Pepare all pizza toppings and place in bowls; cover and chill until party time.

- Arrange flavored syrups and bottles of sparkling water at a beverage station for the Italian sodas. Prepare any garnishes, if using.

THIRTY MINUTES BEFORE THE PARTY

- Preheat the oven to 500°F.

- Remove the dough from the refrigerator at least 20 minutes before rolling; roll into 8-inch rounds and transfer to prepared baking sheets.

- Prepare the Tossed Salad—toss with dressing just before serving.

- Top and bake 2 pizzas on each of 3 baking sheets, rotating pans halfway through baking.

TWENTY MINUTES BEFORE DESSERT

- Sauté the peaches for the Peaches with Lemon Shortbread.

- Set out the ice cream to soften for easy scooping.

ITALIAN SODAS

You've probably seen the bottles of flavored syrups that line the walls of coffeehouses or cafés. They are used to make flavored coffee, tea, and cocktails, and can also be used in cooking and baking. Kids love to make their own sodas, so buy assorted syrup flavors in small bottles. Torani is a readily available brand.

To make Italian sodas, simply add 2 tablespoons of the flavored syrup to 8 ounces of sparkling water in an ice-filled glass. Offer colorful straws—even paper umbrellas—and garnishes like fresh fruit to up the fun factor.

MAKE-YOUR-OWN PIZZA

Serves 4 to 6; yields 6 crusts

½ cup warm water

2¼ teaspoons active dry yeast

4 to 4½ cups unbleached bread flour

1½ teaspoons kosher salt

1 teaspoon sugar

1¼ cups water at room temperature

2 tablespoons extra-virgin olive oil

While packaged prepared pizza crusts and refrigerated dough are readily available (and a totally acceptable convenience), it's fun to have a homemade pizza crust recipe in your repertoire. The ingredients are cheap, the dough is simple to make, and it freezes well. You will need 3 large (17 × 13-inch) baking sheets to make six individual pizzas at a time.

1. Combine the warm water and yeast in a small glass bowl. Let stand 5 minutes.

2. Place the flour, salt, and sugar in the bowl of a stand mixer fitted with the paddle attachment and mix to combine. Add the yeast mixture, the room-temperature water, and 2 tablespoons of the olive oil and mix on low speed for 1 minute. Switch to the dough hook and mix on medium speed for 5 minutes, or until the dough is smooth and elastic.

3. Transfer the dough to a large oiled bowl; turn it to coat the top of the dough. Cover with plastic wrap and let stand for 1 to 1½ hours, or until doubled in bulk.

4. Punch down the dough and divide it into 6 equal pieces. (If not using immediately, transfer the balls to resealable plastic bags and refrigerate up to 3 days or freeze up to 6 months.) Cover the dough with plastic wrap and let it stand 20 minutes.

5. Preheat the oven to 500°F.

6. Drizzle 1 tablespoon of olive oil on each of 3 baking sheets. (If using a pizza stone, preheat in the oven for 30 minutes. It will be very hot!) Roll or press the pizza dough into 8-inch circles and transfer 2 circles of dough to each of 3 baking sheets. Brush the remaining 3 tablespoons of olive oil over the surface of each dough round. Spoon Monday Night Marinara Sauce (recipe follows) over each, leaving a 1-inch border. Top with desired pizza toppings.

7. Transfer two of the baking sheets to the bottom rack of the oven and the remaining baking sheet to the top rack. Bake the pizzas for 10 to 12 minutes, or until the crust is golden brown and the cheese is bubbly, rotating the pans halfway through. Remove the pans from the oven and let the pizzas rest 2 to 3 minutes before slicing.

OUR FAVORITE TOPPINGS

Mozzarella

Parmigiano-Reggiano

Garlic

Pepperoni

Ham

Pineapple

Goat cheese

Green pepper

Jalapeños

Fresh basil

Sliced black olives

Chopped spinach

MONDAY NIGHT MARINARA SAUCE

Makes about 5 cups

1 tablespoon extra-virgin olive oil

1 sweet onion, such as Maui or Vidalia, diced

Pinch of kosher salt

4 garlic cloves, minced

2 tablespoons chopped fresh oregano

2 28-ounce cans crushed San Marzano tomatoes

¼ teaspoon red pepper flakes

Pinch of sugar (optional)

¼ cup chopped fresh basil

This sauce is quick to throw together any night of the week, then it just requires a slow, hands-off simmer to let the flavors really come together. San Marzano tomatoes are a variety of Italian plum tomato known for their sweet flavor and low acidity. Quality canned tomatoes are such a great convenience for making homemade tomato sauce, and San Marzano tomatoes are the best of all. Double this recipe and freeze a batch for later.

1. Heat the olive oil in a large saucepan over medium-high heat. Add the onion and a pinch of salt and sauté until soft and translucent, about 8 minutes. Add the garlic and oregano and sauté 2 minutes more. Add the tomatoes with their juice to the pan with the red pepper flakes.

2. Bring the sauce to a boil, reduce the heat to low, and simmer, partially covered, for 30 to 45 minutes. Taste the sauce from time to time, adding more seasoning to taste. If you like a sweeter sauce, add a pinch of sugar.

3. Turn off the heat and stir in the fresh basil. At this point the sauce is perfect for pasta. For pizza, if you prefer a smoother consistency, carefully puree the sauce in the pot with an immersion blender or transfer to a blender and puree until smooth. Taste and adjust seasoning one more time before serving or freezing.

"*Shared meals are our family tradition.*"

Tip: When blending hot liquids in a blender, leave ample space at the top, as the liquid will expand. Hold down the top firmly as you turn it on.

TOSSED SALAD WITH LEMON-PARMESAN DRESSING

Serves 6

A crunchy green salad is the perfect pizza pairing and I like to keep it simple!

Tear 3 romaine hearts from one package into pieces and place them in a large salad bowl with 1 cup of seasoned croutons. Combine ¼ cup freshly squeezed lemon juice, 1 teaspoon finely grated lemon zest, 1 tablespoon grated Parmigiano-Reggiano, one smashed garlic clove, and a healthy pinch of kosher salt and freshly ground black pepper in a jar with a lid. Shake vigorously, then set it aside for 10 minutes. Pour in ⅔ cup extra-virgin olive oil and shake well or whisk to emulsify. Remove the garlic clove before tossing the salad with the dressing.

PEACHES WITH LEMON SHORTBREAD

Serves 6

1 cup (2 sticks) unsalted butter, softened, plus 3 tablespoons

½ cup confectioners' sugar

1 teaspoon lemon zest

1 teaspoon vanilla extract

¼ teaspoon kosher salt

2 cups all-purpose flour

6 firm-ripe peaches, peeled (see page 212), pitted and cut into wedges or halves as desired

4 tablespoons packed light brown sugar

Ground cinnamon

Vanilla ice cream

The crunch of cookies and the creaminess of ice cream with warm, caramelized peaches are a pretty amazing combo. Consider crumbling the cookies over the peaches if you prefer.

1. Preheat the oven to 350°F.

2. Line two baking sheets with parchment paper. In a large bowl, beat 1 cup of the butter until creamy with an electric mixer. Add the confectioners' sugar and lemon zest and beat until smooth. Beat in the vanilla. Add the salt and stir in the flour, a little at a time, mixing until just combined. Form the dough into a 10-inch-long log; wrap it tightly in plastic and freeze until firm, 30 minutes (or up to 1 month).

3. Slice the dough into ¼-inch-thick slices. Place the cookies on the prepared baking sheets and bake 25 to 30 minutes, or until the cookies are slightly browned around the edges. Let them cool on the pan 5 minutes, then transfer them to wire racks to cool completely.

4. In a large saucepan, melt the remaining 3 tablespoons butter over medium heat. Add the brown sugar and stir until melted. Add the peach wedges and cook, stirring, until the sugar is fully dissolved and the peaches are soft and warmed through. Sprinkle with cinnamon.

5. To serve, scoop the ice cream into bowls. Top with equal amounts of the sautéed peach wedges and serve with 1 or 2 shortbread cookies.

MISTLETOE AND MARTINIS—
A HOLIDAY OPEN HOUSE

Menu

CRANBERRY MARGARITA MARTINI

MULLED CIDER

CLASSIC HERSHEY'S HOT COCOA

CJ'S ORANGE CRANBERRIES AND ROSEMARY PECANS

GARLIC-ROASTED SHRIMP COCKTAIL

CHICKEN AND SMOKED SAUSAGE GUMBO

SOUTHWESTERN CORN CHOWDER

CORNBREAD WITH GREEN CHILIES AND PEPPER JACK CHEESE

SPICED ZUCCHINI BREAD

TRIPLE CHOCOLATE CRANBERRY OATMEAL COOKIES

LEMON COCONUT BARS

HELLO DOLLIES

PEANUT BUTTER INCREDIBLES

Serves 10 to 12

Christmas is such a magical time of year. I love everything about it—from the music to the food, to wrapping presents. And there are so many good smells! Whether it's cookies baking, the Christmas tree, or my pot roast in the oven on Christmas Day, I love it when the house is filled with wonderful aromas.

We have certain traditions at Christmastime that I hope my girls will pass on to their own families one day. My in-laws have given me pieces of the Spode Christmas Tree china pattern since John and I were married twenty-six years ago. I have a big enough collection now to give my daughters sets of their own someday. Starting around December 1, we trade in our regular plates and mugs for the Spode Christmas china. It signals the beginning of the Christmas season in our house.

We also go as a family to choose a live tree each year. Once the tree is inside, the Christmas decorations come down from the attic, we queue up the Christmas music, and drink hot chocolate in front of the fire while we decorate the tree.

Most of our ornaments have a personal story behind them. Each of my girls gets an ornament for Christmas every year (I love the idea that they will have a nice collection of ornaments when they begin Christmas traditions in their own homes), and there are several that my grandmother made for me as a child. We also try to bring home a memento or ornament to hang on the tree from each trip we take as a family. So trimming the tree also becomes an opportunity to share stories and reminisce about times we have spent together.

When I was a child, Santa Claus always covered the presents under the tree with a bedsheet or blanket. Then my dad would do the "big reveal" on Christmas morning as we all stood and watched. Each of us had a specific area under the tree where all our presents from Santa were placed. Santa does the same thing at my house to this day.

Every year I make Chicken and Smoked Sausage Gumbo on Christmas Eve and sometimes we all go to a movie. One year we saw *It's a Wonderful Life* at a small independent theater in Nashville called the Belcourt. It was so fun seeing it in a real theater on the big screen! When we came outside after the movie, there were huge, beautiful snowflakes falling. It looked just like a scene in the movie! I always wish for a white Christmas, and that year the whole town was covered in a thick and glistening white blanket of snow when we woke up on Christmas morning.

I also love the holiday season because it is the perfect excuse for entertaining. Sure it's a busy time of year and a popular time for parties (yes, you might have some competition), but I find that an open house allows friends to pop by on their way home from shopping or on the way to or from another party to have a bite, visit a little, and then get on to other plans with ease. I created this cocktail party menu so that most everything can be made ahead of time.

When I first gave this party a few years ago, I invited more than 100 people! The invitation read:

PLEASE COME CELEBRATE THE SEASON WITH US.

WE KNOW IT'S A BUSY TIME OF YEAR,

WHETHER YOU HAVE 10 MINUTES OR 4 HOURS . . .

WE WOULD JUST LOVE TO SEE YOUR FACE!

This let them know they didn't have to commit to an entire evening and alluded to the come-and-go vibe of an open house. Since there was no way I could keep up with drinks for 100 people, I hired a bartender. Hiring help is definitely a splurge, but it's worth it for a crowd like this. You can hire a professional (I asked the bartender from a favorite restaurant) or enlist the help of a friend, relative, or neighbor who mixes a great drink.

Plan this to be as big and festive or as small and intimate as you like. I think a good number to invite is 25 to 30 people so that the house is always full and never feels empty or lifeless. You want your guests to feel like they are walking into a party! But don't limit yourself—if you have lots of friends and are up to it, bump up your numbers and scale the recipes for as many people as your house can hold!

For this party, I originally offered three different takes on the martini: a classic vodka martini, a Manhattan martini, and a margarita martini. This year I offered a festive red spin on a margarita mixed with cranberry. Serve what you enjoy—a green apple martini, a cosmopolitan, or a lemon drop. I always include red wine, white wine, and beer, too. Champagne is fitting for this particular party. Set up a Champagne station with iced Champagne, glasses, and fresh raspberries for guests to help themselves. I scatter a few tea lights around, and the table looks gorgeous and classic. Just be sure to include plenty of nonalcoholic options—and water. It's such a busy time of year and as a host I am always grateful that this party gives me the opportunity to fill my home with close friends and family to toast another holiday season.

As you can see, this party has a *lot* of recipes and food, but, as always, feel free to tailor the menu any way that works for you. Make only one of the soups. Make cider *or* cocoa. Skip the dip. Make this into a dessert party entirely. Do whatever makes you feel comfortable, confident, and happy.

my holiday playlist

1. "What Christmas Means to Me" (Stevie Wonder)

2. "Sleigh Ride" (Ella Fitzgerald)

3. "Santa Claus Is Back in Town" (Elvis)

4. "The Christmas Song (Merry Christmas to You)" (Nat King Cole)

5. "Do You Hear What I Hear" (Whitney Houston)

6. "It's the Most Wonderful Time of the Year" (Andy Williams)

7. "Have Yourself a Merry Little Christmas" (Frank Sinatra)

8. "Christmas (Baby Please Come Home)" (Darlene Love)

9. "Christmas Time Is Here" (Vince Guaraldi Trio)

10. "Happy Xmas (War Is Over)" (John Lennon)

CHRISTMAS CHEER + HOLIDAY SHIMMER + EASY SELF-SERVE SETUP

A holiday open house should feel warm, cozy, and festive. Open houses are a great way to see a lot of people and have time to spend with everyone. I find it's a much more relaxed atmosphere than a seated dinner or a cocktail party in a tight time frame. If the party falls on a weekend, plan to have the open house during the day and into the early evening, or on a weekday, set the time for early in the evening, as people are coming home from work. It's helpful to define a time frame on the invitation: "Come join us for a Christmas open house from 5:30 to 8:00" (or 2:00 to 5:00 . . . whatever suits your schedule). If you want to keep the party going longer, you can, but this lets everyone know that there is a window of time that they can stop by.

As far as decorating goes, this party is an easy one, because typically your house will already be decorated for the holidays—or it forces you to get your act together and deck the halls! Make your entryway or an area by the front door warm and welcoming. This is your guests' first impression of your party, so give it the same attention as you give the rest of the house.

Tip: It's nice to send people home with something like homemade cookies, a small bag of CJ's Orange Cranberries and Rosemary Pecans mix (page 117), or paperwhite narcissus bulbs. Package any of these in cellophane with a pretty ribbon or gift tag and arrange the gifts on a tray near the front door for guests to grab on their way out.

A wreath or garland on the porch, a twinkling Christmas tree in the living room, and fresh greenery on the mantel or stair banister are holiday touches that make any home festive and inviting. Order holiday greenery in advance, either for local pickup or online for delivery a few days before the party. Request that garlands, wreaths, and flowers be delivered about five days before the party so they are fresh and fragrant. I like my house to glow, so I use lots of candles, including nice holiday-scented ones to make the house smell like Christmas and add to the holiday atmosphere.

I change out my regular throw pillows for Christmas ones during the holidays. Look for fun or decorative ones that suit your style. A bowl of pretty Christmas ornaments—silver and gold, red and green, or even light blue, whatever goes with your decor—is an inexpensive and easy way to add festive sparkle to a table.

Don't forget to make a playlist of Christmas music, both classics and modern tunes. I like the music to be just loud enough that people have to speak up a bit, which adds to the excitement level, but not so loud that people have to yell to be heard.

One of the hardest things for me is having a place for people to put their coats and purses. I don't want to put a big rolling rack in my entryway, as I feel like that messes up the feel of the party. But a small rack or bench near the front door where people can place their coats and bags is a thoughtful touch. It also looks nicer than coats thrown on the backs of furniture all over your house!

Expect that some people will bring gifts. It's helpful to designate a small table near the front door for people to set bottles of wine and other gifts that they bring you.

SANITY SAVER

Two words: Party rental! People at a come-and-go, stand-up affair often forget where they set down their plate or glass, so they simply grab new ones. For that reason, count on two glasses per person for this party. Sure you can buy or borrow glasses, but rental glasses make life easier for the host because all you have to do is rinse and return them. I like stemless wineglasses because they can be used for every type of drink and are sturdier than delicate stemware. You may wish to do the same for bowls and plates, too.

"You want your guests to feel like they are walking into a party!"

Tip: "Open house" should not mean guests wandering freely into your bedroom, closets, or home office. We all have off-limits spaces where we throw stuff or stash things on the day of the party. For me it's our master bedroom and bathroom. I make sure these spaces are either locked, dark, or have something like a chair in front of the door to signal that it's not okay to peek or venture further. Advice I read once in a party book stuck with me: People will snoop! It's human nature. So, it's wise to make sure that the medicine cabinet or top drawer of your bathroom vanity doesn't have anything in it that you wish kept secret!

COOKING GAME PLAN

TWO WEEKS BEFORE THE PARTY

- Make the Cranberry Simple Syrup and refrigerate.

THREE DAYS BEFORE THE PARTY

- Prepare and completely cool CJ's Orange Cranberries and Rosemary Pecans and store in an airtight container.

- Prepare the Triple Chocolate Cranberry Oatmeal Cookie dough, cover, and chill.

- Prepare the Spicy Cocktail Sauce with Red Onion, cover, and chill.

TWO DAYS BEFORE THE PARTY

- Prepare the Lemon Coconut Bars through Step 5 of the recipe. Wrap and refrigerate the cooled pan.

- Chop the onion, celery, and bell pepper for the Chicken and Smoked Sausage Gumbo and store in resealable plastic bags in the refrigerator.

- Chill all beverages (beer, white wine, Champagne, etc.).

ONE DAY BEFORE THE PARTY

- Slice the fruit and measure the spices for the Mulled Cider, place in resealable plastic bags, and chill.

- Chop the onion, bell pepper, celery, and chilies for the Southwestern Corn Chowder, and place in resealable plastic bags. Cook the bacon (reserving the fat), wrap, and refrigerate.

- Prepare the Chicken and Smoked Sausage Gumbo. Cool and refrigerate.

- Prepare the Spiced Zucchini Bread. Cool, wrap, and store the loaves at room temperature.

- Mix the Cranberry Margarita Martini in a large pitcher. Skewer cranberries for garnish (if using), wrap, and chill.

- Prepare the Garlic-Roasted Shrimp Cocktail. Cover and chill.

- Prepare the Southwestern Corn Chowder. Cool and refrigerate.

- Bake the Triple Chocolate Cranberry Oatmeal Cookies, cool, and store in an airtight container.

- Make Peanut Butter Incredibles and Hello Dollies; cover and keep at room temperature.

MORNING OF THE PARTY

- Cut lime wedges for the Cranberry Margarita Martini, cover, and chill. Salt/sugar the martini-glass rims.

- Place 2 to 3 tablespoons of Spicy Cocktail Sauce with Red Onion in each serving glass for the Garlic-Roasted Shrimp Cocktail.

- Prepare the Cornbread with Green Chilies and Pepper Jack Cheese and cool.

- Complete the Triple Chocolate Cranberry Oatmeal Cookies.

- Complete the Lemon Coconut Bars.

TWO HOURS BEFORE THE PARTY

- Reheat the Chicken and Smoked Sausage Gumbo over low heat in a slow cooker or chafing dish.

- Unwrap and slice the zucchini loaves, arrange on a serving tray, and cover with plastic.

- Make rice for the Chicken and Smoked Sausage Gumbo, fluff with a fork, and let stand at room temperature.

ONE HOUR BEFORE THE PARTY

- Place three shrimp on each shrimp cocktail glass, garnish, and chill until the party. If serving a crowd, place the shrimp on a platter.

- Reheat the Southwestern Corn Chowder in a slow cooker or on the stovetop, and transfer it to a chafing dish (if using). Reheat the bacon for 1 minute in the microwave, cool, and crumble. Chop cilantro as garnish.

FORTY-FIVE MINUTES BEFORE THE PARTY

- Make the Classic Hershey's Hot Cocoa. Transfer the cocoa to a thermal carafe (if using). Serve with marshmallows and whipped topping on the side, if desired.

- Prepare the Mulled Cider and transfer it to thermal carafes (if using) just before the party. Provide cinnamon sticks for garnish and dark rum for spiking, if desired.

CRANBERRY MARGARITA MARTINI

Makes 12 4-ounce cocktails, plus extra cranberry simple syrup for guests who prefer a sweeter cocktail

For the cranberry simple syrup:

1½ cups fresh or thawed frozen cranberries

1 cup sugar

2 tablespoons grated orange zest

½ cup fresh orange juice

½ cup water

½ cup ice cubes

For the cocktail:

¾ cup fresh lime juice

1½ cups fresh orange juice

2¼ cups tequila

1½ cups cranberry simple syrup

This is a martini, if only for the glass in which it's served. Cranberry syrup is a colorful cocktail infusion for the holidays, especially when cranberries are so abundant. Stock up now, because they keep in the freezer up to nine months. When it's party time, serve this in a pitcher placed in an ice-filled bowl or bucket so the drink can be served "up" chilled without ice. Provide stirrers for each martini glass, extra ice, and a cocktail shaker on the bar so guests can shake, strain, and serve themselves a perfectly chilled cocktail.

1. For the cranberry simple syrup: Combine the cranberries, sugar, orange zest, orange juice, and the water in medium saucepan. Cook on medium-low heat, stirring frequently, for 10 to 12 minutes, or until the cranberries start to burst and the sugar is dissolved. Pour the cranberry mixture through a fine-mesh strainer into a glass container, gently pushing the cranberry mixture against the mesh of the strainer with the back of a wooden spoon. Add the ice cubes and stir. Chill in the refrigerator for at least three hours.

2. For the cocktail: Combine the lime juice, orange juice, tequila, and 1 cup of the cranberry simple syrup in a large pitcher, stirring to mix. Chill the cocktail mixture for at least 2 hours. Serve aside the remaining simple syrup, so guests can sweeten to taste.

For the glasses:

6 tablespoons
kosher salt

6 tablespoons sugar

12 lime wedges

Lime twists (optional)

Skewered fresh
cranberries (optional)

3. For the glasses: Combine the salt and sugar in a small shallow bowl or on a plate. Wet the rims of 12 5-ounce martini glasses by rubbing with the lime wedges. Lightly press the rim of each glass into the salt-sugar mixture while slowly turning the glass so that only the outer edge is covered. Drop in a lime wedge.

4. To serve, pour ½ cup of the stirred cocktail mixture into the prepared glasses and garnish with lime twists and skewered cranberries, if desired. You can also shake the mixture in an ice-filled (not crushed ice) cocktail shaker before straining into the prepared glasses to make sure it's very cold.

DIAL IT UP

If you want to really highlight the martini theme, set up a station with pitchers of premixed—stirred-not-shaken—martinis (page 147) using 5 parts gin (the classic martini) or vodka (my personal favorite!) to 1 part vermouth. Offer an array of "splashes" like fruit juices, bitters, even olive brine (for dirty martinis) and garnishes such as twists of citrus peel, fresh cranberries, olives, and pickled onions for guests to create their own signature martinis. Be sure to have plenty of toothpicks and cocktail stirrers for the full effect, and keep the pitchers on ice to ensure your martinis will stay cold. Cheers!

MULLED CIDER

Makes 1 gallon

1 gallon fresh-pressed
apple cider

3 medium oranges,
thinly sliced

2 lemons, thinly
sliced

5 cinnamon sticks,
plus more for garnish
(optional)

2 teaspoons whole
cloves

¾ teaspoon allspice
berries

Dark rum for spiking
(optional)

Mulled cider is simply cider simmered with warm spices like clove and cinnamon and often fruit. I like the familiar Christmassy flavor of allspice, too. Just use what you like in small doses . . . you can always add more to taste as the cider simmers. I'm all about the way my house smells when people arrive, and this does the trick for creating a warm, holiday aroma to greet guests when they walk through the door.

1. Bring the cider to a boil in a large stockpot over high heat with the orange and lemon slices, cinnamon sticks, cloves, and allspice, then reduce the heat to low and simmer for 30 minutes.

2. Strain the cider and keep it warm. Add rum to taste, if desired. Add a cinnamon stick to each mug, if desired.

Note: If you don't have all the spices in your pantry or simply to make your party prep easier, look for packets of mulling spices at the grocery store and follow the instructions on the package.

CLASSIC HERSHEY'S HOT COCOA

Serves 5 (8-ounce servings)

½ cup sugar

¼ cup Hershey's cocoa

Dash of kosher salt

⅓ cup water

4 cups milk

¾ teaspoon vanilla extract

2 cups miniature marshmallows or sweetened whipped topping (optional)

This tried-and-true recipe for hot chocolate comes straight from the back of the cocoa tin. Make it and serve it in a thermal carafe on the dessert table so guests can help themselves. This recipe is easily doubled.

1. Stir together the sugar, cocoa, and salt in a medium saucepan; stir in the water. Cook over medium heat, stirring constantly, until the mixture comes to a boil. Boil and stir for 2 minutes. Add the milk, reduce the heat to medium-low, and cook, stirring constantly, until heated through. Do not boil.

2. Remove from the heat; add the vanilla. Beat with a rotary beater or whisk until foamy. Serve topped with marshmallows or whipped cream, if desired.

COFFEE WITH "EXTRAS"

I like to have a coffee station with freshly brewed coffee kept warm in a thermal carafe. Arrange the cups and saucers on a console or counter and provide the usual sweeteners and cream alongside. For this party, I included a tray with bottles of Baileys Original Irish Cream, Irish whiskey, and Kahlúa alongside for guests who like their coffee with a little Christmas cheer!

CJ'S ORANGE CRANBERRIES AND ROSEMARY PECANS

Makes 6 cups

3 cups (24 ounces) raw pecan halves

3 cups orange-flavored cranberries, such as Ocean Spray or Trader Joe's brand

½ tablespoon extra-virgin olive oil

1½ tablespoons minced fresh rosemary

½ teaspoon coarse sea salt (optional)

My friend CJ gave me these one year for Christmas and I begged her for the recipe. These are addictive—crunchy, chewy, salty, and sweet all rolled into one. CJ says you can alter this recipe to fit your tastes, such as by adding a bit of cracked black pepper or cayenne pepper for a spicy twist.

1. Preheat the oven to 425°F.

2. Place the pecan halves on a 17 × 13-inch rimmed baking sheet and toast for 6 to 8 minutes, or until golden brown and fragrant. Remove from the oven and let cool.

3. Mix together the cranberries and the pecan halves in a large bowl. Drizzle with the olive oil and sprinkle with the rosemary and sea salt, tossing to coat.

GARLIC-ROASTED SHRIMP COCKTAIL

Serves 10 to 12

3 pounds jumbo tail-on shrimp (16 to 20 or 21 to 25 count), peeled and deveined

8 garlic cloves, finely chopped

4 tablespoons extra-virgin olive oil

1½ teaspoons kosher salt

¾ teaspoon cracked black pepper

2 tablespoons fresh lemon juice

On an abundant food table like the one for this party, I like to portion things on the smaller side, so people get to sample lots of different things without feeling stuffed. Spoon a little of the cocktail sauce in the bottom of a small aperitif glass or brandy snifter, then hang 2 to 3 shrimp on the side of the rim that guests can dunk as they please. Of course you can also arrange the shrimp on a platter with a bowl of cocktail sauce in the middle. Just be sure to serve them with tails on and keep them cold by placing them in large bowls of crushed ice. This is especially important if the shrimp will be sitting out for most of the party.

1. Preheat the oven to 450°F.

2. In a large bowl, combine the shrimp, garlic, olive oil, salt, pepper, and lemon juice. Spread the shrimp in a single layer on a 17 × 13-inch rimmed baking sheet lined with parchment paper.

3. Roast the shrimp for 6 to 8 minutes, turning once, or until they are opaque and firm. Transfer the shrimp to a shallow dish and refrigerate, partially covered, for at least 3 hours. Serve with Spicy Cocktail Sauce with Red Onion (recipe follows).

SPICY COCKTAIL SAUCE
WITH RED ONION

Makes 2 cups

1 cup ketchup

1 cup chili sauce

¼ cup grated red onion

1 teaspoon finely chopped fresh jalapeño

6 tablespoons prepared horseradish

2 tablespoons fresh lemon juice

1 tablespoon Worcestershire sauce

¼ teaspoon kosher salt

Dash of Tabasco hot sauce (optional)

Combine the ketchup, chili sauce, onion, jalapeño, horseradish, lemon juice, Worcestershire sauce, salt, and Tabasco, if desired, in a medium bowl. Chill, covered, until ready to use.

CHICKEN AND SMOKED SAUSAGE GUMBO

1 cup vegetable oil

1 cup all-purpose flour

1½ cups chopped yellow onion

1 cup chopped celery

1 cup chopped green bell pepper

1 pound smoked sausage such as andouille or kielbasa, cut crosswise into ½-inch-thick slices

¼ teaspoon cayenne pepper

3 bay leaves

8 cups chicken stock or canned low-sodium chicken broth (I like Campbell's)

1 pound boneless smoked or roasted chicken breast, cut into ½-inch chunks

9 cups cooked long-grain white rice

Finely chopped flat-leaf parsley for garnish

Serves 10 to 12

John and our girls love this recipe, but all praise should go straight to Emeril Lagasse. I make this often for special occasions. Just be warned: This recipe requires a lot of stirring! It's the sort of recipe to make when you have plenty of time to spare. The longer you cook the roux, the deeper the flavor. Just be careful not to burn it or the gumbo will be bitter. Personally, I like to cook the roux really slow and aim for a rich chocolate color. The key is to have all your ingredients chopped and prepared before you start. I use sausage from a local Nashville BBQ restaurant and bake unseasoned chicken breasts covered with chicken broth (which I use later in the gumbo) and foil in a 350°F oven for about an hour.

1. Heat the oil in a large pot or Dutch oven over medium heat. Add the flour and cook, stirring slowly and constantly with a wooden spoon, to make a dark brown roux the color of dark chocolate, 20 to 25 minutes. (Be careful when stirring as the oil is boiling hot!)

2. Add the yellow onion, celery, and bell pepper and cook, stirring, until soft, 5 minutes. Add the sausage, cayenne, and bay leaves and cook, stirring, for 5 minutes. Add the stock and stir until the roux mixture and stock are well blended, and bring to a boil.

3. Reduce the heat to low and cook at a very low simmer, uncovered, stirring occasionally, for 1 hour. Add the chicken, stir, and simmer, stirring occasionally, for 2 hours.

4. Remove from the heat and discard the bay leaves. Taste and adjust the seasoning. Serve over cooked white rice and garnish with parsley, if desired.

SOUTHWESTERN CORN CHOWDER

Serves 10 to 12

8 slices thick-cut
applewood-smoked bacon,
cut into
1/2-inch pieces

1 medium yellow onion,
diced

1 medium red bell pepper,
chopped

2 celery stalks, chopped

2 fresh, small poblano
chilies, seeded and cut
into 1/4-inch dice

1/2 teaspoon kosher salt

1 1/2 teaspoons ground
cumin

1/2 teaspoon freshly
ground black pepper

1/8 teaspoon cayenne
pepper

1 1/2 cups dry white wine
or chicken stock

Corn chowder is such a satisfying soup. Creamy and savory, it hits the spot. I like this version's Southwestern take.

1. Cook the bacon 6 to 8 minutes in a large Dutch oven, over medium heat, stirring occasionally, until crisp. Remove the bacon with a slotted spoon and drain on paper towels. Drain the fat, reserving 4 tablespoons.

2. Add the reserved bacon fat and onion to the Dutch oven and cook over medium heat for 4 minutes, or until tender. Add the bell pepper, celery, and chilies and cook until softened, about 5 minutes. Add the salt, cumin, black pepper, and cayenne pepper. Increase the heat to high and add the wine. Cook until most of the liquid has evaporated, 3 to 5 minutes.

3. Add the potatoes and chicken stock and bring to a boil. Reduce the heat to medium-low and simmer until the potatoes are tender, about 25 minutes. Stir in the corn.

1½ pounds Yukon Gold potatoes, peeled and cut into ½-inch cubes

6 cups low-sodium chicken stock

3½ cups fresh or frozen corn kernels (about 12 ears if using fresh)

1 cup heavy cream

¼ cup all-purpose flour

¼ cup chopped fresh cilantro, plus more for garnish

4. In a medium bowl, combine the cream and flour, stirring with a whisk to create a slurry. Add the slurry to the Dutch oven and cook over medium-low heat, stirring frequently, for 8 to 10 minutes or until slightly thickened. Stir in the cilantro. Garnish with cilantro and reserved bacon pieces, crumbled.

CORNBREAD WITH GREEN CHILIES AND PEPPER JACK CHEESE

5 tablespoons unsalted butter, melted, plus 2 tablespoons for greasing the pan

1½ cups whole buttermilk

1½ cups milk

4 large eggs

⅔ cup vegetable oil

3 cups all-purpose flour

1 cup stone-ground yellow cornmeal

⅔ cup sugar, plus 2 tablespoons for dusting

2 tablespoons baking powder

1 teaspoon kosher salt

¼ teaspoon coarsely ground black pepper

1 4-ounce can diced green chilies, drained

1 cup (about 4 ounces) shredded pepper jack cheese

Serves 10 to 12

I'm always looking for a good cornbread recipe that isn't too dry. This is the best I've found so far.

1. Preheat the oven to 350°F. Generously grease a 13 × 9-inch baking pan with the 2 tablespoons of butter.

2. Combine the buttermilk, milk, eggs, oil, and melted butter in a large bowl. Combine the flour, cornmeal, ⅔ cup of the sugar, baking powder, salt, and pepper in a large bowl.

3. Add the buttermilk mixture to the flour mixture, stirring until just combined. Stir in the green chilies and the pepper jack cheese. Pour the batter into the prepared pan. Sprinkle the remaining 2 tablespoons of sugar over the batter.

4. Bake for 40 to 45 minutes, or until a wooden toothpick inserted into the center comes out clean.

SPICED ZUCCHINI BREAD

Makes two 9-inch loaves

2 cups all-purpose flour

3 teaspoons ground cinnamon

1 teaspoon kosher salt

1 teaspoon baking soda

1 teaspoon ground allspice

1½ teaspoons baking powder

1½ cups granulated sugar

1 cup packed light brown sugar

1½ cups vegetable oil

3 large eggs

1 tablespoon vanilla extract

2 teaspoons lemon zest

2½ cups coarsely grated zucchini (about 2 medium)

This bread is so *yummy! Check it with a toothpick after 50 minutes and then keep checking it until the toothpick comes out clean. Emma and I like ours cold with butter on it! My girls don't care for nuts in bread, but if you do, simply add 1 cup of toasted pecans or walnuts when you add the zucchini. This is another recipe that you may wish to double for a crowd.*

1. Preheat the oven to 325°F. Grease and flour two 9 × 5-inch metal loaf pans.

2. Combine the flour, cinnamon, salt, baking soda, allspice, and baking powder in a medium bowl to blend. Whisk the granulated sugar, brown sugar, oil, eggs, vanilla, and lemon zest in a large bowl to blend. Stir the flour mixture into the sugar mixture. Stir in the zucchini and walnuts, if desired. Pour the batter into the prepared pans.

3. Bake for 1 hour and 15 minutes, or until a wooden toothpick inserted into the center of the breads comes out clean. Remove from the oven and let stand for 10 minutes. Then turn the loaves out onto a wire rack and let them cool completely.

TRIPLE CHOCOLATE CRANBERRY OATMEAL COOKIES

Makes 32 cookies

1 cup all-purpose flour

½ teaspoon baking soda

½ teaspoon ground cinnamon

¼ teaspoon kosher salt

10 tablespoons (1¼ sticks) unsalted butter, softened

½ cup granulated sugar

½ cup packed light brown sugar

1 large egg

1 teaspoon vanilla extract

1 tablespoon orange zest

1 cup old-fashioned oats

½ cup semisweet chocolate chunks

As I've said before, I'm not a great baker. But every once in a while I get the urge to bake or make cookies with Ava. This is a holiday twist on the oatmeal cookie. The orange and cranberry take it to a whole new level! Double or triple this recipe depending on how large a crowd you expect or if you're packaging these as party favors. The prepared dough keeps well, covered, in the refrigerator. Let it sit at room temperature for about 20 minutes, then scoop and bake.

1. Preheat the oven to 350°F. Line two 17 × 13-inch rimmed baking sheets with parchment paper.

2. Whisk together the flour, baking soda, cinnamon, and salt in a medium bowl and set aside. In a large bowl, beat the butter, granulated sugar, and brown sugar with an electric mixer until smooth and fluffy. Add egg, vanilla, and orange zest and beat until blended. Add the flour mixture and oats and stir until blended. Stir in the chocolate chunks, ½ cup of the milk chocolate chips, ½ cup of the white chocolate chips, and the cranberries.

1 cup milk chocolate chips

1 cup white chocolate chips

½ cup dried cranberries

3. Drop the batter by rounded tablespoons onto the prepared baking sheets, at least 2 inches apart. Bake for 12 to 14 minutes, or until the edges are lightly browned. Cool on the sheets for 5 minutes, then transfer the cookies to a rack and cool completely.

4. In separate small bowls, microwave the remaining ½ cup milk chocolate chips and ½ cup white chocolate chips at high power for 1 minute, stirring after 30 seconds. Using a small spoon, drizzle the melted chocolate over the cookies. Let stand until the chocolate sets, about 1 hour. (Can be made 2 days ahead. Store in an airtight container at room temperature.)

LEMON COCONUT BARS

Makes 30 bars

For the crust:

2 cups all-purpose flour

½ cup sugar

½ teaspoon kosher salt

1½ cups sweetened flaked coconut, toasted (see Note)

12 tablespoons (1½ sticks) chilled, unsalted butter, cut into ½-inch cubes

For the filling:

1½ cups sugar

4 large eggs

2 tablespoons finely grated lemon zest

½ cup fresh lemon juice

2 teaspoons all-purpose flour

1 teaspoon baking powder

Pinch of kosher salt

⅓ cup confectioners' sugar

Delaney loves lemon bars, so I set out to find a really good recipe to have on hand. These are great, and the dusting of confectioners' sugar seems like a little dusting of snow! Make these up to 2 days before the party, but don't dust with the confectioners' sugar until just before guests arrive.

1. For the crust: Preheat the oven to 350°F. Line a 13 × 9-inch baking pan with foil, leaving a 1-inch overhang on all sides. Lightly grease the foil.

2. Combine the flour, sugar, and salt in a food processor; blend for 5 seconds. Add the coconut and butter; process until the mixture resembles fine meal and begins to clump together. Gather the dough into a ball, and press it evenly into the prepared pan.

3. Bake for 15 to 20 minutes, or until the crust is golden around the edges.

4. For the filling: Combine the sugar, eggs, lemon zest, lemon juice, flour, baking powder, and salt in a food processor and blend until smooth.

5. Pour the filling evenly over the hot crust. Return the pan to the oven and bake for 25 to 30 minutes, or until the filling begins to brown at the edges and is just set. Transfer the pan to a wire rack and let it cool completely.

6. Using the foil as an aid, transfer the lemon bars to a work surface. Flatten the foil edges. Cut into 30 (3 × 1-inch) bars. Sift confectioners' sugar over the bars.

Note: To toast coconut, spread flakes in a single layer in a skillet and cook over medium heat, stirring frequently, until golden. Transfer to a plate to cool quickly. Sweetened coconut will toast faster than unsweetened coconut, so watch carefully.

HELLO DOLLIES

Makes 16 servings

1 stick unsalted
butter, melted

1 cup graham cracker
crumbs

1 14-ounce can Eagle
Brand sweetened
condensed milk

1 cup flaked
sweetened coconut

1 cup semi-sweet
chocolate chips

1 cup butterscotch
chips

These delicious bars are just as simple as it gets. I got this recipe from my mother-in-law, Flavia McBride. She always made these for John—this is his favorite dessert!

1. Preheat the oven to 350°F.

2. Pour the melted butter into an 8-inch square baking pan. Spread the graham cracker crumbs on top of the butter in the bottom of the pan. Pour the sweetened condensed milk over the crumbs and top with a layer of coconut, a layer of chocolate chips, and a final layer of butterscotch chips.

3. Bake in the preheated oven for 30 minutes. Alternatively, microwave uncovered on medium-high for 10 minutes.

4. Let it cool and cut into 2-inch squares.

PEANUT BUTTER INCREDIBLES

Makes 36 (2 ⅛ × 1 ½-inch) bars

⅔ cup unsalted butter

1 cup chunky peanut butter (I like Jif)

2 cups confectioners' sugar

1½ cups fine graham cracker crumbs

1¼ cups semisweet chocolate chips

1 cup butterscotch chips

If you love the peanut-butter-and-chocolate combo like me, this is a winner. It's also super easy and a good recipe if baking isn't your strong suit. But be forewarned—these are addictive! I always make them at Christmastime for my friend Paul Worley (we've made many records together). He happens to make the best sweet pickles, so at Christmas, it's a pan of these for him and a jar of pickles for me and we're both happy!

1. Grease a 13 × 9-inch baking dish.

2. Melt the butter in a medium saucepan over low heat. Stir in the peanut butter until smooth. Add the sugar, then the graham cracker crumbs, and stir well to blend. Press the mixture over the bottom of the prepared baking dish.

3. Melt the chocolate chips and the butterscotch chips in a bowl in the microwave on high in 30-second increments, stirring each time, for a total of 2½ minutes, or until the chocolate-butterscotch mixture is melted and smooth. Pour the melted chocolate over the crumbs and spread evenly. Refrigerate until the topping has set. Slice into bars and store at room temperature.

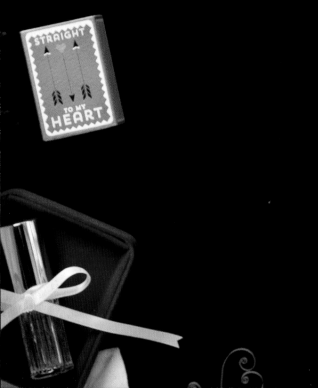

RETRO VALENTINE'S DAY SUPPER CLUB

Menu

VODKA MARTINI

BACON-WRAPPED STUFFED DATES

HERB-AND-CHEESE SPIRALS

ICEBERG WEDGE SALAD

STUFFED TWICE-BAKED POTATOES

FILET MIGNON WITH THYME BUTTER
AND SHERRY MUSHROOMS

ASPARAGUS WITH TOASTED ALMONDS

CHOCOLATE-DIPPED STRAWBERRIES

Serves 6

If you haven't been part of a supper club, you're missing out. Supper clubs can consist of a set group of friends or an ever-changing crowd. You can meet monthly (like we do) or quarterly at your home, or rotate houses. You set the rules, but however you do it, supper clubs are a perfect way to ensure you keep up with friends and always have something to look forward to on your calendar. When it's your turn to host, you can create and prepare the entire menu, or divvy up recipes for dishes your guests should bring. I prefer rotating houses because it gives each host an opportunity to set the scene. Preparing the entire menu when it's your turn allows you to express yourself and your personal tastes, plus I like how it adds an element of surprise for your guests.

When I think "retro" I think fashion. Elizabeth Montgomery in *Bewitched* and my mother in old photos come to my mind. I grew up on a farm in Kansas, where things were simple. I was never really exposed to anything fancy or city-like, but I do remember my mom dressed up occasionally in shifts and heels with her hair and makeup done. She was so glamorous . . . like Natalie Wood. I treasure a photo from one of my childhood birthday parties where she is looking so on-trend for the time in a jumpsuit with her hair pulled into a high bun. I thought she was the most gorgeous, exotic thing I had ever seen. I love the fact that she dressed up like that for my brother's third and my fifth birthday (we share a birthday two years apart) and with no one to see her but my dad, sister and brothers, and our grandparents. Her effort to dress up shows what a spark and sense of style she had. To me, she always looked like a movie star. When I get ready for this retro dinner, I always get my inspiration from her!

Tip: *This dinner takes some choreography, so use my Cooking Game Plan to help you navigate the process. I try to keep the cocktail window to about 40 minutes when serving rich nibbles and stiff drinks like classic martinis. You don't want your guests to get stuffed or have two martinis before dinner and fall face-first into their iceberg wedge! Guests always seem to congregate in the kitchen, so enlist their help. This is a supper club, after all! Everyone can chat and sip martinis while helping plate the salads, warm the serving plates, and garnish the cake.*

Supper club themes to build on are infinite and can be so fun. Here's my list: Havana Nights, Tapas from Spain, Bollywood, Evening in Athens, When in Rome, Black and White, '70s TV-Tray Dinner (in front of the TV), Oscar Night (or Golden Globes . . . Grammys), Moulin Rouge, A Night in Paris, The Best of Julia Child, New Orleans/Mardi Gras, Crab Boil, BBQ, Roaring '20s, Silent Movie Night, Grapes of Wrath, Midwestern Casserole Extravaganza, Game Night, Poker Night/Las Vegas, and Wine Country. Find inspiration from movies, shows, novels, songs, you name it!

my retro valentine's playlist

1. "Mack the Knife" (Bobby Darin)

2. "All of Me" (Billie Holiday)

3. "Moon River" (Audrey Hepburn)

4. "A Wink And A Smile" (Harry Connick Jr.)

5. "At Last" (Etta James)

6. "Unforgettable" (Nat King Cole)

7. "Fly Me to the Moon" (Julie London)

8. "What A Wonderful World" (Louis Armstrong)

9. "Fever" (Peggy Lee)

10. "The Way You Look Tonight" (Frank Sinatra)

RED ROSES ✚ VALENTINES ✚ VINTAGE FINDS

I like giving homemade valentines . . . like the kind you made in third grade. So I loved the idea of having each guest make a homemade valentine for their sweetie to bring the night of the party to be used as place cards on the table. Each guest writes the name of their date on the front of the valentine and a personal message on the inside (which should not be shared until dessert). To make the project easy, I mailed all the craft supplies needed as part of the invitation. A printed card with the party details went inside a white letter-sized padded envelope or a box filled with red and pink construction paper, a glue stick and glitter glue, sequins, beads, and paint pens along with directions for what to do. You could also use the boxed, store-bought valentines kids give to classmates, but homemade ones are fun, personal, and add a touch of kitsch that's fitting for this retro theme.

A vintage bar cart is perfect here. Or, outfit a large, high-sided tray set on a table or sideboard with martini glasses, a cocktail shaker, ice bucket, napkins, toothpicks, and stirrers. Since there used to be one on every table, consider dusting off—and washing well—a collection of old ashtrays. You can find them cheap at secondhand stores. Give them new life as dishes for nuts and olives, or simply as a place for discarded toothpicks. A box or two of candy cigarettes on side tables is a playful nod to old (hopefully) habits.

This party is all about style and fashion. Since "retro" might mean the 1980s to twenty-somethings and the 1930s to a much older group, it's important to define the era and the dress code in the invite. Tell guests to don their finest clothes à la *Mad Men* or *Bewitched*, and let the era dictate your food and playlist choices, too.

I decorated with red, white, and black with gold accents. Because it's the perfect choice for Valentine's Day, I splurged on lots of red roses. I arranged lots of roses in low vases down the center of the table with classic taper candles in candelabras mixed in. A cluster of blooms in a bud vase dressed up the bar top.

Tip: To save money, I get flowers from my local grocery. If there is a wholesale florist in your area, that can keep costs down, especially if you're buying lots of one kind of flower.

"A party favor is a token reminder of the evening."

Keep dishes and linens plain and neutral or just use what you have. Clean lines were all the rage in the fifties and sixties, so simple white dinnerware and cotton napkins work perfectly. But funky, mod shapes and patterns are good choices, if you have them. The homemade valentines as place cards add a lot to the table, too.

If a party favor is a token reminder of the evening, choose one that would be a memento of the era being celebrated. I ordered small sample-sized bottles of classic perfumes—Chanel No. 5 and Shalimar—online for the ladies and put them in velvet ring boxes to suggest a Valentine's Day jewelry surprise. You don't have to do this exactly. The key is to make the favors special and beautiful. For the men, small flasks engraved with a single initial, a skinny tie, even cuff links with hearts are other retro ideas that fit the bill.

COOKING GAME PLAN

TWO DAYS BEFORE THE PARTY

- Prepare the Thyme Butter and chill.

- Make the dressing for the Iceberg Wedge and chill.

- Trim the asparagus and slice the shallots for the Asparagus with Toasted Almonds; cover and store in the refrigerator.

- Slice the mushrooms for the Filet Mignon with Thyme Butter and Sherry Mushrooms; cover and store in the refrigerator.

ONE DAY BEFORE THE PARTY

- Make the Stuffed Twice-Baked Potatoes through Step 4, wrap, and refrigerate.

- Stuff and wrap the Bacon-Wrapped Stuffed Dates and refrigerate.

- Combine the filling for the Herb-and-Cheese Spirals; cover and chill.

MORNING OF THE PARTY

- Chill the salad plates.

- Prepare the Herb-and-Cheese Spirals through Step 4 and chill.

- For the Iceberg Wedge Salad, cut the lettuce into wedges, quarter the tomatoes, cook and crumble the bacon, and chop the chives. Cover and refrigerate.

- For the Chocolate-Dipped Strawberries, dip the strawberries in chocolate and refrigerate.

THREE HOURS BEFORE THE PARTY

- Blanch and shock the asparagus; drain.

ONE HOUR BEFORE THE PARTY

- Remove the steaks from the refrigerator, bring to room temperature, and season.

- Prepare the Asparagus with Toasted Almonds through Step 2.

- Bake the Herb-and-Cheese Spirals and cool on a rack.

THIRTY MINUTES BEFORE THE PARTY

- Bake the Bacon-Wrapped Stuffed Dates; keep warm.

- Sear the steaks (Step 3 of Filet Mignon with Thyme Butter and Sherry Mushrooms) and set aside; preheat the oven.

- Sauté the mushrooms (Step 4 of Filet Mignon with Thyme Butter and Sherry Mushrooms).

WHEN GUESTS ARRIVE

- Bake the Stuffed Twice-Baked Potatoes.

- Make the Vodka Martinis to order and set out the Herb-and-Cheese Spirals and the Bacon-Wrapped Stuffed Dates.

FIFTEEN MINUTES BEFORE DINNER

- Finish the steaks in the oven.

- Finish the Asparagus with Toasted Almonds as the steaks cook; keep warm.

- Complete the Sherry Mushrooms for the Filet Mignon with Thyme Butter.

- Plate the Iceberg Wedge Salads.

VODKA MARTINI

I learned how to make a proper martini from a connoisseur of sorts, my dear friend Dave Stewart from Eurythmics. He and I have shared many of these chilled gems, and he agreed to let me share his method with you. While a classic martini is made with gin, I'm a vodka girl. Cheers!

To make the perfect martini, make sure the vodka is *very* cold. It's best kept in the freezer. You must have hard ice cubes. Crushed ice will melt when the martini is shaken, causing your drink to be diluted. Place 3 olives on a cocktail skewer/stirrer and place in a martini glass. Add a splash of dry vermouth over the olives and swirl it around the glass. Place the vodka in a cocktail shaker filled with hard ice. Shake vigorously for about 30 seconds. Pour the vermouth out of the martini glass. Strain the vodka into the glass with the olives.

—*Dave Stewart*

Sipping a Dave Stewart specialty

BACON-WRAPPED STUFFED DATES

Serves 6

¼ cup plus
1 tablespoon of goat
cheese, softened

1 tablespoon fresh
thyme leaves

¼ teaspoon freshly
ground black pepper

15 whole Medjool
pitted dates

30 lightly salted
roasted whole
almonds (about
¼ cup)

5 slices bacon, cut
crosswise into thirds

Wooden picks
(at least 30)

2 tablespoons
balsamic glaze
(optional, see
Headnote)

I dare you to eat just one of these! If you want a hint of acidity to cut the richness of the bacon and cheese, drizzle with a glaze made by slowly simmering ½ cup of balsamic vinegar until it has reduced by half and is syrupy. Bottled balsamic glaze or reduction is also available where you find vinegars and oils in the grocery store nowadays.

1. Preheat the oven to 375°F.

2. Combine the goat cheese, thyme, and pepper in a small bowl.

3. Cut each date in half crosswise, then cut a lengthwise slit in each piece. Stuff each date half with ¼ teaspoon of the goat cheese mixture and 1 almond. Pinch the dates closed. Wrap each date securely in a piece of bacon and secure with a wooden pick. (These may be wrapped and refrigerated up to 1 day before baking.) Arrange the dates, seam side down, on a wire rack set on a 17 × 13-inch baking sheet.

4. Bake for 24 to 26 minutes, or until the bacon is browned and crisp. Serve warm or at room temperature. Drizzle with the balsamic glaze, if desired.

HERB-AND-CHEESE SPIRALS

Makes 32 spirals

8 ounces goat cheese, softened

¼ cup finely grated Asiago

1½ teaspoons minced fresh garlic

2 tablespoons snipped chives

1 teaspoon freshly ground black pepper

1 17.3-ounce package of puff pastry

½ teaspoon sea salt

Freshly grated Parmigiano-Reggiano

These savory bites are based on palmiers, the French butterfly-shaped pastries. They are flaky and buttery. Since this is a rich meal, I decided to cut the formed dough down the middle to halve the butterflies and create smaller, bite-sized nibbles perfect for cocktails. They are elegant and go so well with a dry martini.

1. Preheat the oven to 400°F.

2. Combine the goat cheese, Asiago, garlic, chives, and pepper in a small bowl.

3. Unroll one pastry sheet on a lightly floured surface and roll it into a 10 × 12-inch rectangle. Spread the cheese mixture evenly over the pastry (I use my fingers).

4. Roll up the pastry evenly from each short side, meeting in the middle of the rectangle. Slice through the space where the two rolls meet to create 2 separate spiral logs. Freeze for 20 minutes.

5. Remove the pastry from the freezer and cut each log into 16 slices. Arrange the slices on parchment-lined baking sheets, sprinkle evenly with the sea salt and freshly grated cheese, and bake for 20 to 22 minutes, or until golden-brown.

ICEBERG WEDGE SALAD

Serves 6

For the dressing:

1 cup good-quality blue cheese, softened

½ cup whole buttermilk

½ cup sour cream

¾ cup mayonnaise

1½ tablespoons apple cider vinegar

¼ teaspoon kosher salt

¼ teaspoon freshly ground black pepper

For the salad:

2 small heads iceberg lettuce

2 cups quartered heirloom cherry tomatoes

8 slices bacon, cooked and crumbled

3 teaspoons chopped chives, divided

1 tablespoon chopped flat-leaf parsley

Iceberg lettuce gets such a bad rap, but it's super-refreshing and really holds up well for a party. And with this being a retro party, it makes sense to use iceberg instead of our more evolved leafy greens. I think chilling salad plates is as important as warming dinner plates. Just stack the salad plates in the fridge the morning of the party.

1. Combine the blue cheese, buttermilk, sour cream, mayonnaise, vinegar, salt, and pepper in a medium bowl, whisking until thoroughly combined.

2. Quarter each head of lettuce and reserve 2 quarters for another use. To serve, place a wedge of lettuce on each salad plate. Top with the blue cheese dressing, tomatoes, bacon, chives, and parsley.

STUFFED TWICE-BAKED POTATOES

Serves 6

3 medium russet
potatoes, scrubbed

3½ tablespoons
unsalted butter, at
room temperature

½ cup crème fraîche
or sour cream, at
room temperature

¼ cup half-and-half,
warmed

Kosher salt, to taste

Freshly ground black
pepper, to taste

2 tablespoons
snipped fresh chives

These potatoes are old-school favorites that are great for dinner parties because they are easily made ahead and chilled or frozen.

1. Position the oven rack in the center of the oven and preheat to 350°F.

2. Pierce the potatoes several times and set them directly on the oven rack. Bake until tender all the way through, 1½ hours. Transfer the potatoes to a work surface and set aside 10 to 15 minutes, or until cool enough to handle.

3. Slice each potato in half lengthwise, cutting cleanly rather than sawing so as to not tear the skin. Using an oven mitt to protect your hand from the heat, hold a potato half in one hand and gently scoop out the flesh with a spoon, leaving ¼ to ½ inch of potato in the shells. Repeat with the remaining halves.

4. Force the flesh through a potato ricer or mash it with a potato masher and transfer to a mixing bowl. One at a time, stir in 3 tablespoons of the butter, the crème fraîche, and the half-and-half using a wooden spoon. Season the potatoes with salt and pepper to taste. Carefully scoop the filling into the potato skins, compacting it lightly. Top each with bits of the remaining butter. (Potatoes can be refrigerated overnight at this point or frozen for up to 3 months.)

5. Preheat the oven to 350°F. Arrange the potatoes on a baking sheet or in a large baking dish. Bake until heated through and beginning to brown in spots on top, 20 to 25 minutes (30 to 35 minutes if made ahead and refrigerated; for frozen potatoes, cover in foil and bake for 45 minutes, then uncover and bake for 15 minutes more). Let the potatoes rest for 10 minutes, then garnish with the snipped chives to serve.

Tip: I actually have good luck with making the potatoes in the microwave. Use the baked potato setting on your microwave (or cook on high for 6 to 8 minutes). Just be sure to pierce the scrubbed potatoes a few times, then watch closely so that they do not get overcooked. They are done when you can stick a fork all the way through.

FILET MIGNON WITH THYME BUTTER AND SHERRY MUSHROOMS

Serves 6

¾ cup (1½ sticks)
unsalted butter,
softened, plus
6 tablespoons

1 tablespoon chopped
fresh thyme

6 6-ounce filets
mignons, 1½ inches
thick

1 tablespoon, plus
½ teaspoon kosher
salt

2 tablespoons
coarsely cracked
black pepper

¼ cup extra-virgin
olive oil

3 cups sliced
baby portobello
mushrooms

2 garlic cloves, finely
chopped

¾ cup sherry

¼ teaspoon freshly
ground black pepper

I won't lie . . . beef tenderloin is expensive. I recently made a steak dinner when my daughter's boyfriend was eating with us for the first time because she said, "He loves steak! Make steak, Mom!" How could I resist? The receipt for seven filets was pretty shocking. There are less expensive and more flavorful cuts, but none is as meltingly tender. Others worth trying are top sirloin and tri-tip steaks.

1. Combine the ¾ cup of butter and the thyme in a medium bowl and mix until the thyme is well incorporated. Transfer the butter to a sheet of plastic wrap and form it into a 4-inch log. Roll it up in the plastic wrap and chill for at least 1 hour or up to 4 days in advance.

2. Preheat the oven to 400°F.

3. Season the steaks generously with 1 tablespoon of the salt, or to taste, and the cracked black pepper on both sides. Heat 2 tablespoons of the olive oil in a large cast-iron skillet over medium-high heat. Cook the steaks in 2 batches, searing 2 minutes per side until well-browned, adding about 1 tablespoon of oil for each batch. Remove the skillet from the heat. Transfer the steaks to an ovenproof, rimmed baking sheet and place in the oven. Cook for 8 to 10 minutes for medium-rare (145°F) or 12 to 14 minutes for medium (160°F).

4. While the steaks are finishing in the oven, add 2 tablespoons of the butter to the skillet and return it to the burner. Add the mushrooms and cook over high heat, stirring frequently, until golden-brown around the edges, 6 to 8 minutes. Remove the mushrooms from the skillet and set aside.

5. Add the garlic and ½ cup of the sherry to the skillet, stirring to loosen any browned particles from the bottom. Return the skillet to the heat and, being careful that the sherry does not flame up, cook until it is reduced by half, 2 to 3 minutes. Add 2 tablespoons of the remaining butter, stirring to combine. Add the reserved mushrooms to the pan and season with the remaining ½ teaspoon of salt and the freshly ground pepper. Remove from the heat and whisk in the remaining 2 tablespoons of butter and the remaining ¼ cup of sherry. Serve the mushrooms over the steaks and top with a ½-inch-thick slice of thyme butter.

SANITY SAVER

If searing steaks while guests are underfoot seems daunting, cook a 4-pound beef tenderloin butt (the thicker end of a beef tenderloin) instead. Ask your butcher to remove the silver skin for you. Rinse and pat the loin dry and let it come to room temperature for 30 minutes. Season the meat all over with salt and pepper and sear it on all sides in a large, blasting-hot cast-iron skillet with a few tablespoons of olive oil (this is a great time to use your vent hood!). Transfer the browned meat to a rack set over a roasting pan, insert a meat thermometer, and roast in a preheated 450°F oven until the internal temperature registers 140°F, approximately 20 minutes. Remove the pan from the oven and let the meat rest 15 minutes before slicing. Serve with the Thyme Butter and Sherry Mushrooms prepared as above. Leftovers make the best roast beef sandwiches!

ASPARAGUS WITH TOASTED ALMONDS

Serves 6

⅓ cup sliced almonds

1½ pounds fresh asparagus spears, ends trimmed

1 tablespoon extra-virgin olive oil

1 large shallot, thinly sliced lengthwise

2 tablespoons unsalted butter

¼ teaspoon kosher salt

¼ teaspoon freshly ground black pepper

Whenever I'm planning a dinner party, I like to have some super-simple sides like steamed vegetables that come together quickly and require minimal prep. This recipe is a great example. The ends of asparagus can be woody and tough. Just snap them off where they naturally break before you cook the spears.

1. Heat a small, dry skillet over medium heat and toast the almonds for 3 to 4 minutes, shaking the pan regularly, until light golden brown. Transfer to a plate to cool quickly.

2. Fill a large bowl with ice and water. Bring a large pot of generously salted water to a boil. Add the asparagus and let the water return to a boil. Cook 2 to 4 minutes, depending on thickness, until bright green and crisp-tender. Drain and plunge the asparagus into the ice water to shock, or stop the cooking.

3. Heat ½ tablespoon of the olive oil in a large sauté pan over medium heat. Add the shallot and cook until it begins to brown. Turn heat to low, add 1 tablespoon of the butter, and cook 8 to 10 minutes, or until very soft and evenly browned, stirring often. Remove the shallot from the pan with a slotted spoon and set aside.

4. Turn the heat to medium-high and add the remaining ½ tablespoon of oil and the asparagus to the pan. Cook for 3 to 5 minutes, turning often, until heated through. Add the remaining tablespoon of butter, and the salt and pepper, tossing the asparagus to coat as the butter melts.

5. Place the asparagus on a warm serving platter and sprinkle with the reserved shallot and toasted almonds.

CHOCOLATE-DIPPED STRAWBERRIES

Serves 6 to 8 (3 or 4 strawberries per person)

1 cup bittersweet chocolate chips

1 tablespoon shortening

4 cups small fresh strawberries with tops

About as fitting an ending for a Valentine's Day feast as you can get, these chocolate-covered berries are a cinch to make. You could also melt white chocolate chips and offer both kinds arranged on a pretty plate to enjoy with after-dinner coffee.

1. Place the chocolate and shortening in a 2-cup glass measuring cup. Microwave on high at 30-second intervals, stirring after each interval, until the chocolate is melted and smooth.

2. Holding the strawberries by the stems, dip them in the chocolate, leaving a little red around the top, and let the excess chocolate drip back into the cup. Transfer the chocolate-covered berries to a parchment-lined baking sheet.

3. Refrigerate at least 30 minutes, until the chocolate is set.

SPRING BRUNCH OUTDOORS

Menu

DIY MIMOSA BAR

BLOODY MARY BAR

VEGGIES AND DIP

CAPRESE SALAD

OVEN-COOKED BACON

CHERRY-ROSEMARY MUFFINS

YOGURT PARFAIT

ZUCCHINI, SUN-DRIED TOMATO, AND BASIL TART

SCALLOPED POTATOES

MINI HAM-AND-CHEESE BISCUITS WITH APPLE JELLY

Serves 10 to 12

When Delaney was maybe three years old, John and I decided we needed a weekend getaway, just the two of us (which I highly recommend, by the way). We took a trip to New Orleans and had such a great time wandering the French Quarter, stopping in restaurants to enjoy the great Cajun food and shopping for antiques on Magazine Street. One thing that was highly recommended to us was brunch at Brennan's. Wow—it was amazing! I will never forget sipping a mimosa, looking at the menu, and thinking, This is living! I had grillades and grits, which is sautéed veal served in a seasoned Creole sauce over savory grits. It's a New Orleans classic and was absolutely delicious. After lingering over the meal, we walked around some more, and then went back to the hotel for a nap—proof that brunch is relaxing! It was a day I'll never forget, and I try to re-create that lazy-day feeling with not a care in the world whenever I'm hosting a brunch.

Because it's slower-paced and usually enjoyed on weekends when no work-day plans can keep friends from lingering, brunch naturally has a relaxed feel. The fun often lasts well into the afternoon, which feels kinda like you're playing hooky by tossing the day's to-do list out the window. Plus, what's not to love about sipping Champagne in the middle of the day? I've found that the secret to a good brunch is to offer a mix of dishes that are traditionally served for breakfast with options that are considered more lunchtime fare. It's the combination that makes it interesting.

While I have hosted brunches all times of the year, I think they are especially nice outdoors in springtime when the weather is warm, the flowers are blooming, and the birds are singing. The world is waking up from a long winter nap. We all are a bit stir-crazy by the time spring rolls around so being outside is like a breath

of fresh air. Literally! So if a beautiful morning inspires you to host a spur-of-the-moment brunch, just go for it. Some of the best times I've ever had involved calling friends to come over at the last minute to share a meal and a beautiful day. Good friends don't care if everything is perfect. They just want to be with you. If you've planned ahead, whip up this brunch menu. If not, have someone grab a box of doughnuts and a dozen eggs on the way over and make do. And always, always have a bottle of Champagne and some OJ in your fridge . . . you never know when you might need it!

Recently, I hosted a brunch that was a bit more elaborate than just having a few friends over. Delaney was graduating from high school and we talked about what kind of gathering she wanted to have to celebrate her big day. The graduation ceremony was in the afternoon so we decided a brunch beforehand would be nice. Relatives were in from out of town and, as luck would have it, the day was gorgeous. I scaled the recipes to feed a crowd. Delaney is kind of a free spirit and doesn't like things to be too fussy, so for the tables I created loose arrangements of mixed spring flowers picked up from the grocery store that I filled in with mint, lavender, rosemary, and basil from the yard. They smelled great, fit her personality, and felt like springtime.

Keep the weather in mind when planning a party outdoors, because it can be unpredictable. In Tennessee we have a few days of beautiful weather between the many days of spring showers. The pretty days usually catch me off guard and by the time I plan something it's raining again. So prepare for last-minute raindrops or sudden winds and have a Plan B in your back pocket, which means it's

just as important to prep your inside spaces for this party. If everyone has to move inside, you want to make sure there are plenty of places to sit and to rest plates.

Brunch can be one of the more challenging meals to orchestrate because there are so many things that have to be ready to serve at the same time. And since this is an earlier-in-the-day occasion, you don't have the whole day to cook! I encourage you to use the make-ahead tips suggested in the Game Plan.

Send guests home with a little something. Line a wooden berry basket with a pretty napkin filled with goodies like fresh biscuits, a small jar of jelly or jam, and fresh, ripe strawberries for a sweet send-off after a memorable gathering.

my brunch
playlist

1. "Hallelujah I Love Her So" (Ray Charles)

2. "Baby I Love You" (Aretha Franklin)

3. "Stealing" (Gavin DeGraw)

4. "I Shall Be Released" (Maroon 5)

5. "Easy" (Commodores)

6. "Brand New Day" (Van Morrison)

7. "Stronger" (Faith Hill)

8. "King of the Road" (Roger Miller)

9. "Angel From Montgomery" (Bonnie Raitt)

10. "Son of a Preacher Man" (Dusty Springfield)

HOMESPUN EASE ✚ SPRING BLOSSOMS ✚ PASTELS AND BRIGHT HUES

While I like the idea of hosting a relaxed, laid-back catch-up with friends where everyone makes a plate and plops down wherever they feel comfy, I also love the idea of my friends relaxing around a pretty table and having lingering conversations. So just go with what feels right. When I'm serving food outside buffet-style, I think it's always a good idea to cover dishes with mesh domes or other covers to keep hungry bugs and flies off the food. I often set the buffet up inside . . . either on my island, kitchen table, or sideboard . . . and let guests fill their plates and then wander outside.

Spring is unpredictable temperature-wise, so it's nice to have a few throws that guests can wrap around their shoulders or cover their laps with to take away the chill. I like how branches with forced blooms add height and a pretty spring touch to the DIY Mimosa and Bloody Mary Bars. This is the kind of party where you can really let your individual sense of style show. An all-pastel palette is pretty for spring, but bright bold colors can work as well. Weaving the two together adds interest. Metal chairs in different colors add a funky touch. I always like using real plates and glasses and cloth napkins to make gatherings feel special. But feel free to mix and match dishes and linens or go the classic route and match everything up. Choose a vibe—retro, shabby chic, or elegant—and go with it. I'm of the opinion that as long as you put some effort into creating a cohesive look, you will be setting the stage for a memorable day no matter what style you choose.

SANITY SAVER

Saturday or Sunday morning is a time when most people want to have a family day and babysitters aren't readily available. So if you are inviting guests who have kids, it's good to have a few kid-friendly foods (pigs in a blanket are loved by guests both big and little!) and maybe some activities and toys to keep them entertained. If the day stretches into the afternoon, having a few kid movies at the ready is also a great idea.

"Good friends don't care if everything is perfect. They just want to be with you."

COOKING GAME PLAN

TWO DAYS BEFORE THE PARTY

- Chill the Champagne, vodka, and Bloody Mary mix.

ONE DAY BEFORE THE PARTY

- Measure or cut all garnishes for the Bloody Mary and DIY Mimosa Bars and store (in serving containers if possible).

- Wash and cut the vegetables and make the red cabbage bowl for the Veggies and Dip and chill.

- Bake the Cherry-Rosemary Muffins.

- Chop and slice the vegetables for the Zucchini, Sun-Dried Tomato, and Basil Tart.

- Assemble the Yogurt Parfaits except for the granola and honey, and chill.

MORNING OF THE PARTY

- Place juices for the DIY Mimosa Bar in serving containers and chill.

- Bake tea biscuits for the Mini Ham-and-Cheese Biscuits with Apple Jelly; slice the cheese and ham.

- Assemble and bake the Zucchini, Sun-Dried Tomato, and Basil Tarts.

- Combine the Bloody Mary mix and vodka, place in serving pitchers, and chill until serving.

ONE HOUR BEFORE THE PARTY

- Prepare the Oven-Cooked Bacon, cool, and place on a serving platter.

- Slice, assemble, and bake the Scalloped Potatoes.

- Arrange the Veggies and Dip and fill the cabbage bowl with the dip. Cover until serving.

THIRTY MINUTES BEFORE THE PARTY

- Top the Yogurt Parfaits with the granola and honey.

- Arrange Mini Ham-and-Cheese Biscuits on a serving platter and place the apple jelly and Dijon mustard in serving bowls.

- Arrange the Bloody Mary and DIY Mimosa Bars with serving pitchers and bowls of garnishes, plus buckets of ice and scoops.

- Arrange the Caprese Salad.

DIY MIMOSA BAR

Let them sip Champagne! And do it any way they like. A mimosa bar is a brunch no-brainer. A few bottles of bubbly, assorted juices, and fresh fruit garnishes and your guests are in biz. Here is a list of mimosa-ready mix-ins. You can do all or just a couple of your favorites.

4 bottles of your favorite Champagne or Prosecco

2 cups pomegranate juice

2 cups lemonade

2 cups blood orange juice

2 cups blackberry juice

2 cups raspberry juice

2 cups pear juice

2 cups mango-pineapple juice

1 cup pomegranate seeds

1 cup fresh blueberries

1 cup fresh blackberries

1 cup fresh raspberries

1 cup diced pineapple

Tip: Take a few flower petals from whatever flowers you choose to decorate with and freeze them with water in ice cube trays. Use the floral ice in the Champagne bucket on the mimosa bar as a pretty flourish.

BLOODY MARY BAR

You know what they say . . . A brunch without a Bloody Mary is just breakfast. Provide the mix, vodka, and lots of garnishes to wow your guests. Use the list below as a jumping-off point. Go ahead and prep and fill bowls with all the garnishes a day ahead. Just cover and refrigerate until it's time to give (or eat) the toast.

1 750-milliliter bottle of vodka

2 32-ounce bottles of Bloody Mary mix (I love Zing Zang)

Garnishes:

1 bunch celery stalks with leaves, trimmed

2 16-ounce jars pickled okra

½ cup cornichons

1 cup green olives

3 lemons, cut into wedges

3 limes, cut into wedges

12 baby carrots, with tops

1 pound (16 to 20 count) cooked, peeled shrimp

½ cup prepared horseradish

1 small bottle hot sauce or Sriracha

2 tablespoons celery salt

2 tablespoons smoked paprika

1 small bottle Worcestershire sauce

pepper grinder

Combine the vodka and Bloody Mary mix in a large pitcher. Chill in the refrigerator until ready to serve. Stir before serving. Serve the Bloody Mary garnishes in bowls, jars, or on platters with serving utensils and skewers.

VEGGIES AND DIP

1 large head purple cabbage

6 medium carrots, cut into 4-inch sticks

6 celery stalks, cut into 4-inch sticks

2 cups heirloom cherry tomatoes

2 English cucumbers, cut into 4-inch sticks

1 bunch radishes, washed and trimmed

1 red bell pepper, seeded and cut into strips

1 green bell pepper, seeded and cut into strips

1 yellow bell pepper, seeded and cut into strips

Hidden Valley Original Ranch Dip Mix dressing (see Box)

A hollowed-out cabbage makes a pretty "bowl" for the dip. All the veggies and the cabbage bowl can be prepped, wrapped, and chilled a day, or even two, before the party. If you can find radishes with tops, it's pretty to leave them on. To serve, simply scoop the dressing into the cavity of the cabbage and replenish as needed. Let your guests munch on the veggies while you finish cooking.

Cut out the stem of the cabbage and remove enough of the leaves to form a bowl. Be sure to leave about a ½-inch layer of leaves to hold the dip. Arrange all the vegetables on a large serving platter around the cabbage bowl. Fill the bowl with the Hidden Valley Original Ranch Dip Mix dressing and serve. Replenish dip as needed.

When it comes to ranch dressing, I have found nothing beats Hidden Valley Original Ranch Dip Mix that comes in envelopes, so I see no point in making it from scratch. Just mix a one-ounce packet of the dip mix with 2 cups of sour cream and chill the dip for a few hours before serving. That's it . . . dip's done!

CAPRESE SALAD

Serves 10 to 12

4 beefsteak or heirloom tomatoes

1 pound mozzarella di bufala

1 bunch basil leaves

2 tablespoons extra-virgin olive oil

2 tablespoons balsamic vinegar (optional)

Sea salt, to taste

Freshly ground black pepper, to taste

Caprese Salad is one of my favorite things in the whole wide world. It's so easy to make and so pretty! I make this for myself for lunch in the summertime at least twice a week. Please, people: Never refrigerate tomatoes! Refrigeration changes their texture, making them mealy.

Slice the beefsteak tomatoes and the mozzarella di bufala. Alternate the tomatoes and cheese, overlapping slightly, in rows, topping each tomato slice with a fresh basil leaf. Drizzle with a few tablespoons olive oil and balsamic vinegar, if desired, and sprinkle lightly with sea salt and freshly ground black pepper. Yum!

OVEN-COOKED BACON

Serves 10 to 12

2 pounds applewood-
smoked bacon

*Nobody wants to be standing over a frying pan when guests
arrive. It's not a cute look. Cooking bacon in the oven is hands-
off simple. It can be prepared in advance by undercooking it
a bit. Just drain, wrap, and refrigerate. Crisp the bacon in the
oven for a few minutes (or microwave in 30-second increments)
until it is done to your liking to serve.*

1. Preheat the oven to 375°F. Line two large, rimmed 17 × 13-inch
baking sheets with aluminum foil or parchment.

2. Lay bacon slices on a baking rack set over the prepared pan in
a single layer and bake for 20 to 25 minutes, or until desired degree
of doneness. Remove the bacon from the pan and place on paper
towels to drain. Serve immediately or wrap in fresh paper towels and
transfer to a resealable plastic bag and refrigerate. Precooked bacon
can be crisped in a hot oven for a few minutes to serve.

Maple–Brown Sugar Bacon (aka "Bacon Candy"): *Bake
1 pound of bacon on a rack set on a baking sheet prepared as above for
15 minutes. Meanwhile, combine ¼ cup Grade A amber maple syrup and
¼ cup packed light brown sugar in a medium bowl. Carefully remove the
bacon from the oven and brush the tops of the slices with the syrup mixture,
then bake 5 minutes more. Carefully remove the bacon from the pan and
place on paper towels to drain. Serve warm. This variation cannot be made
ahead and reheated well.*

CHERRY-ROSEMARY MUFFINS

Makes 24 muffins

4 cups unbleached all-purpose flour

1 teaspoon kosher salt

1½ tablespoons baking powder

1½ cups sugar

2 medium oranges

2 large eggs, beaten

1½ cups milk

½ cup (1 stick) butter, melted

1½ cups dried cherries, lightly chopped

2 tablespoons chopped fresh rosemary

These sweet and savory muffins have a unique and delicious flavor combination.

1. Preheat the oven to 375°F. Lightly grease or line two 12-cup muffin tins.

2. In a large bowl, whisk together the flour, salt, baking powder, and sugar. Grate 2 tablespoons of zest from the oranges and set the zest aside. Then squeeze the oranges to get ½ cup of juice. In a medium bowl, combine the eggs, orange juice, milk, and butter.

3. Stir the egg mixture into the flour mixture, until just combined. Fold in the orange zest, cherries, and rosemary.

4. Spoon the batter into the muffin tins, filling three-fourths of each cup. Bake for 18 to 20 minutes, or until a wooden pick inserted into the center comes out clean.

YOGURT PARFAIT

Makes 10 servings

½ cup blueberries

½ cup raspberries

½ cup quartered strawberries

2 tablespoons sugar

7½ cups vanilla yogurt

1½ cups granola (without raisins)

10 tablespoons honey

If you want to make smaller parfaits, you can adjust the amounts accordingly. It's really all about the layering.

1. Combine the blueberries, raspberries, and strawberries in a medium bowl. Add the sugar. Let stand 20 minutes, stirring occasionally.

2. Place ¼ cup yogurt in the bottom of ten 8-ounce glasses. Top with 2 tablespoons of the berry mixture. Repeat the layers once. Top each serving with ¼ cup of yogurt and sprinkle with 2 tablespoons of granola. Drizzle each with 1 tablespoon honey.

ZUCCHINI, SUN-DRIED TOMATO, AND BASIL TART

Serves 10 to 12

2 frozen deep-dish piecrusts, thawed

3 cups shredded mozzarella

1 cup freshly grated Parmigiano-Reggiano

6 tablespoons crumbled goat cheese

1 cup drained and thinly sliced oil-packed sun-dried tomatoes

1 cup thinly sliced fresh basil

½ cup chopped green onions

2 tablespoons chopped fresh oregano

2 small zucchini, sliced into ¼-inch rounds

4 large eggs

2 cups half-and-half

½ teaspoon kosher salt

½ teaspoon freshly ground black pepper

This savory tart is a favorite in our house. Everyone loves it, especially Delaney, which is why she requested it for her graduation brunch. It has a bit of an Italian flavor with the basil and sun-dried tomatoes, and it looks nice on the brunch buffet, too. The fact that it can be served warm or at room temperature is a bonus. Definitely let it rest for a bit after taking it out of the oven so that it firms up and will be easier to slice and serve. This always goes fast.

1. Preheat the oven to 425°F.

2. Prick the bottom of the crusts with a fork and prebake them for 5 to 8 minutes, or until lightly golden. Reduce the temperature to 400°F. Sprinkle 1½ cups of the mozzarella into each crust, then top each with ¼ cup of the Parmigiano-Reggiano, 3 tablespoons of the goat cheese, ½ cup of the sun-dried tomatoes, ½ cup of the basil, ¼ cup of the green onions, and 1 tablespoon of the oregano. Arrange the zucchini in concentric circles to cover the top of the tart. Whisk together the eggs, half-and-half, salt, and pepper in a medium bowl. Divide the mixture evenly between the piecrusts. Sprinkle each with ¼ cup of the remaining Parmigiano-Reggiano cheese.

3. Bake for 32 to 35 minutes, or until the custard is set and the crust is golden brown. Serve warm or at room temperature.

SCALLOPED POTATOES

Serves 10 to 12

1 tablespoon unsalted
butter

3 cups heavy cream

1 cup milk

6 garlic cloves,
smashed

1 sprig of fresh
rosemary

1 sprig of fresh thyme

3 large sweet
potatoes, peeled and
cut into ⅛-inch-thick
slices

3 large russet
potatoes, peeled and
cut into ⅛-inch-thick
slices

1 cup grated
Parmigiano-Reggiano

¾ teaspoon kosher
salt

¾ teaspoon freshly
ground black pepper

1 tablespoon fresh
thyme leaves

*This recipe is delicious and versatile. It can be made with all
russet potatoes, all sweet potatoes, or a mixture of the two, for a
pretty presentation, as I've done here.*

1. Preheat the oven to 400°F.

2. Generously grease a 13 × 9-inch baking dish with the butter.

3. In a large saucepan, combine the cream, milk, garlic, rosemary,
and thyme. Bring to a low simmer on low heat. Remove from the heat,
cover, and let stand 10 minutes. Remove the garlic, rosemary, and
thyme with a slotted spoon.

4. Spoon 2 tablespoons of the cream mixture into the prepared
baking dish. Layer one-third of the sliced potatoes, alternating the
two colors, in the dish and sprinkle with ⅓ cup of the grated cheese,
¼ teaspoon of the salt, and ¼ teaspoon of the pepper. Repeat layers
twice (the dish will be full). Pour the warm cream over the potatoes
and gently press the potatoes into the cream mixture.

5. Cover with aluminum foil and bake for 55 to 60 minutes, or until
the potatoes are tender. Remove the foil and bake an additional 10
minutes, or until the top is browned. Let stand 10 minutes. Sprinkle
with the thyme leaves.

MINI HAM-AND-CHEESE BISCUITS WITH APPLE JELLY

Makes 24 biscuits

Ham biscuits are a brunch buffet classic. Use whatever style ham and biscuits you like and set out little bowls of mustard and honey, too. The tart-sweetness of apple jelly really pairs nicely with sharp cheddar and salty ham.

Bake 24 frozen tea biscuits, such as Mary B's brand, according to the package directions. Slice 8 ounces of sharp cheddar cheese and 8 ounces of cooked country ham. Halve each biscuit and layer with cheese and ham. Serve with apple jelly and Dijon mustard.

RED, WHITE, AND BLUE COOKOUT

Menu

SPIKED ARNOLD PALMERS

FLAVORED WATERS

ALL-AMERICAN BACKYARD BURGER

GRILLED LEMON SHRIMP

HOT DOGS WITH CLASSIC FIXIN'S

BAKED BEANS

DAD'S MASHED POTATO SALAD

SWEET CORN ON THE COB

RED, WHITE, AND BLUE BERRY SALAD

MOM'S PEACH COBBLER

Serves 10 to 12

We love the Fourth of July around here. Especially John, a borderline fireworks fanatic! A few years ago we went back to my hometown of Sharon, Kansas, to set up a huge fireworks display for the community. It was so much fun that we did it again the next year and it turned into an even bigger celebration with my dad's band, the Schiffters, playing and a huge cookout in the park. The event is right up John's fireworks-crazy alley. With the help of a couple of my nephews and my brother-in-law, he set up a massive display on the ball diamond and the "show" lasted over an hour! It was really fun and we hope to do it again someday.

We are lucky to have a great backyard for entertaining, so that's where we'll be when we are around for the Fourth of July. We have a pool, and I tell people to bring their suits in case they want to cool off, especially the kids! A backyard cook-out is typically a pretty active party with kids running around and friends catching up, so I make it a point to provide plenty of things to do. Lawn games like horse-shoes, croquet, and a beanbag toss are fun for people to join in at their leisure. A piñata is a perfect distraction for the kids. But, don't stop there, a water-balloon toss and potato sack or three-legged races add even more old-fashioned flare.

For Independence Day, I like to serve an all-American menu that represents some of my food traditions growing up—burgers, hot dogs, baked beans, and po-tato salad are mandatory. This is a large menu, so feel free to simplify as you wish. I've tried to include a little something for everyone, but you might not feel like you need all this food. Because it is hot here in the South, I keep all cold foods chilled right up until serving time. Always remember that foods with eggs or mayonnaise can pose a health risk if not handled properly, so it is important to keep them cold. The potato salad can be nestled in a larger bowl filled with ice. Condiments like mayonnaise or dressings can be kept on ice just like the beverages. Personalize foam Koozies; they are great for keeping canned and bottled drinks cool, plus they provide another opportunity to introduce pops of red, white, and blue. Send them home with guests after the party.

Because every city or town has rules about setting off fireworks, I just stock up on the legal, kid-friendly kind, like sparklers, poppers, glowworms, and even smoke bombs for the kids. (If you live in an area where fireworks are allowed, by all means plan your party leading up to a grand finale fireworks display just after dark.) Everyone loves sparklers. I still have fun "writing" words in the air with them. They come in cute retro boxes that not only add to the party decor but also make great favors for guests of all ages. Just be careful to dispose of them after they go out so that little bare feet don't get burned! Stepping on a hot sparkler is no fun. I learned that the hard way. Dispose of them in a bucket of sand or water away from where people are walking.

SANITY SAVER

Pool safety is always critical, but especially so when there is a lot of activity going on and kids are running around. Ask adults to take turns being the "designated lifeguard" so that someone is always monitoring what's going on in the pool. I make sure to provide lots of floating devices—foam noodles, inflatable toys, and rafts—so there is something to grab on to if little swimmers feel fatigued or anyone cares to simply relax and float.

my red, white, and blue cookout playlist

1. "Down On The Corner" (or pretty much any CCR song!)

2. "Jackson" (Johnny Cash and June Carter)

3. "We're an American Band" (Grand Funk Railroad)

4. "American Pie" (Don McLean)

5. "All American Girl" (Train)

6. "American Honey" (Lady Antebellum)

7. "American Woman" (the Guess Who or Lenny Kravitz)

8. "Midnight Train to Georgia" (Gladys Knight & the Pips)

9. "American Girl" (Tom Petty and the Heartbreakers)

10. "Small Town" (John Mellencamp)

PATRIOTIC ACCENTS + ALL-AMERICAN MENU + HOMESPUN CHARM

This is the sort of party where people eat when they're ready and often in shifts, so a buffet setup makes the most sense. A long table positioned against the wall of the house, ideally in the shade, works well. I like to layer the table with a mix of different tablecloths: red, white, and blue solids, checks, or stars and stripes add a patriotic flair. Pinwheels, bunting, and flag accents add to the festivity, plus they are things you can keep using again and again. I grow my stash of decorations by stocking up the week after the Fourth of July when items go on sale in stores and online.

While I always prefer to use "real" dishes, colorful paper or plastic ones are perfectly acceptable for casual outdoor parties like this. Look for red and blue enameled tubs for icing down drinks. I set them at different spots in the yard to make it easy for guests to grab refreshments. So that cans, bottles, and plates don't litter the yard, I always designate an area away from the food table for recycling and trash. Label big trash bins so guests know what goes where and try to keep the lids on so the flies stay away.

Over the years I've collected many things for my ever-growing party pantry, including Mason jars. Once I've used what's inside, I wash and keep the jars. I have lots of them in all different sizes and use them over and over. I guess you could say they are my go-to and can be used for pretty much everything—from holding drinks to holding silverware, to holding flowers, to shielding flickering votives. They are a perfect fit for this party. Plus, they are inexpensive, so you can buy them if you don't have any on hand. String lights are another great idea for adding atmosphere to an evening party, or stuff Mason jars with short strands of battery-powered string lights and tape the battery box to the underside of the jar lid to camouflage it and voilà—you have a fireflies-in-a-jar effect for the table. So pretty!

> *Tip: Mosquitoes are not invited! I make a point to spray outdoor areas a couple of hours before guests arrive and make sure there is no standing water in pots or containers anywhere near where people will gather. Those organic pellets you sprinkle around the yard really work well for controlling mosquitoes and are available at many hardware and gardening stores.*

COOKING GAME PLAN

TWO DAYS BEFORE THE PARTY

- Boil and chill unpeeled eggs for Dad's Mashed Potato Salad.

ONE DAY BEFORE THE PARTY

- Assemble the Baked Beans, cover, and chill.

- Prepare the hamburger mixture and form the patties for the All-American Backyard Burger; cover and chill.

- Make Dad's Mashed Potato Salad.

MORNING OF THE PARTY

- Assemble the Flavored Waters and chill until ready to serve.

- Combine tea and lemonade for Spiked Arnold Palmers and chill.

- Assemble Mom's Peach Cobbler.

TWO HOURS BEFORE THE PARTY

- Cook the Baked Beans.

ONE HOUR BEFORE THE PARTY

- Combine all fruit for Red, White, and Blue Berry Salad; chill.

- Arrange condiments and toppings for All-American Backyard Burger and the Hot Dogs with Classic Fixin's.

- Cut lemons and arrange the bar to serve Spiked Arnold Palmers.

FIFTEEN MINUTES BEFORE THE PARTY

- Marinate shrimp for the Grilled Lemon Shrimp.

AFTER GUESTS ARRIVE

- Complete Mom's Peach Cobbler and bake.

- Grill shrimp, hot dogs, and burgers and toast buns; cover with foil to keep warm.

- Prepare Sweet Corn on the Cob.

SPIKED ARNOLD PALMERS

Serves 10 to 12

2 quarts Sweet Tea (page 196)

2 quarts frozen and reconstituted lemonade

24 ounces (3 cups) bourbon or vodka

2 small lemons, cut into wedges

I love the combination of iced tea and lemonade. It seems so American, especially in the South. Simply leave out the alcohol for an unspiked batch and make sure you clearly label the containers!

In a large pitcher, combine the sweet tea and the lemonade. To serve, pour 8 ounces of the tea mixture over ice and stir in 1 to 2 ounces of bourbon or vodka. Garnish with a lemon wedge.

SWEET TEA

My friend Faith makes the best sweet tea, hands down. Growing up in Kansas, I drank instant tea with white sugar stirred in, and, well, the sugar never really dissolved so you ended up with an inch of white sugar at the bottom of your glass. But we didn't know the difference. Great sweet tea is a true southern tradition, not a midwestern one. So I turned to a good ole Mississippi native to help me with this . . . and it is right! Thanks, Faith!

To make Sweet Tea, fill a 2-quart saucepan three-fourths full with water and bring it to a rapid boil. Pour in just shy of 2 cups sugar and stir until it is completely dissolved. Add 4 family-sized Lipton tea bags (with the paper squares torn off and the strings twisted together so that they stay together). Cover the pan, remove from the heat, and let steep for 20 minutes. Transfer the tea to a 1-gallon pitcher, making sure the tea bags do not fall into the pitcher. Press the tea bags with the back of a spoon to extract any remaining liquid and pour into the pitcher. Discard the tea bags. Add ice water to the pitcher, leaving a 3- to 4-inch space at the top of the pitcher (so it's not entirely full). Stir the pitcher of tea, pour over ice, and drink up! Makes just shy of 1 gallon.

FLAVORED WATERS

Serves 10 to 12

Flavored water is so refreshing, especially on a hot day. I'm not big on sodas—for my kids or me—so I like to have this available as an alternative. Plus it looks so pretty! You can do all or just one of these. Each recipe makes 3 quarts or about enough for 12 guests to have a generous 6-ounce glass of water. Double or triple the recipes as desired.

ROSEMARY-CITRUS WATER

2½ quarts water

2 oranges, thinly sliced

2 limes, thinly sliced

6 strawberries, stemmed and quartered

2 sprigs fresh rosemary, gently crushed

In a 3-quart pitcher, mix the water, oranges, limes, strawberries, and rosemary. Let stand in the refrigerator for at least 4 hours. Serve over ice.

Tip: A rolling pin is the perfect tool for crushing the rosemary so it releases its fragrant oils into the water.

CUCUMBER, LEMON, AND MINT WATER

Serves 10 to 12

2½ quarts water

2 cucumbers, cut into ribbons or sliced

2 small lemons, thinly sliced

2 bunches mint leaves, picked and stems discarded

In a 3-quart pitcher, mix the water, cucumbers, lemons, and 6 mint sprigs. Let stand in the refrigerator for at least 4 hours. Serve over ice and garnish with mint sprigs.

ALL-AMERICAN BACKYARD BURGER

Serves 10 to 12

5 pounds ground chuck (at least 80 percent lean)

3 cups finely chopped spinach (optional)

1 cup chopped sweet onion

3 tablespoons Worcestershire sauce

Kosher salt

Freshly ground black pepper

Vegetable oil for the grill

12 cheese slices (American, Monterey Jack, pepper jack)

12 hamburger buns

Toppings:

Applewood-smoked bacon slices, cooked and halved

Tomato slices

It's no secret I love a good cheeseburger. While there are all kinds of fancy additions and uptown ways to do it, the classic ground beef burger with simple toppings is still my favorite. This is the kind of burger we had growing up and it's the kind my dad still grills on the Fourth.

Feel free to double this recipe if you have more guests. The spinach is totally optional. I like it because it makes the burgers moist and boosts their nutritional value. If you think your guests (especially the kids) are going to freak out over something green in their burger, just chop it really, really fine. They'll never know . . . it can be our little secret.

1. Preheat the grill to medium-high. In a large bowl, mix the ground beef, spinach, onion, Worcestershire sauce, and 3 teaspoons each of the salt and pepper.

2. Divide the meat equally into 12 portions and form into patties about 1 inch thick. Season both sides of the patties lightly with salt and pepper.

3. Lightly brush the grill grates with vegetable oil and place the patties on the grates. Grill the patties for 4 to 5 minutes, then flip and grill 4 minutes more for medium. Place a slice of cheese on top

Green leaf lettuce
leaves

White onion slices

Dill or sweet and
spicy sliced pickles
(I like Wickles Pickles
brand)

Ketchup

Yellow mustard

Mayonnaise

of the patties and cook an additional 1 minute, or until melted. Toast
the buns (if desired), cut sides down, 30 seconds to 1 minute, or until
lightly toasted.

4. Serve burgers with desired toppings.

GRILLED LEMON SHRIMP

Serves 10 to 12

1 cup extra-virgin olive oil

½ cup fresh lemon juice

6 garlic cloves, minced

¼ cup chopped fresh oregano, plus extra for garnish

2 teaspoons kosher salt

2 teaspoons freshly ground black pepper

2 pounds large shrimp (26 to 30 count per pound), peeled and deveined with tails attached

6 lemons, cut into wedges

Another great way to serve this dish is to grill lemon halves, cut sides down, while the shrimp cooks. The lemons get pretty grill marks and become warm and juicy so it's really easy to squeeze them over the shrimp. You will need six lemons to ensure each guest gets a grilled lemon half. Arrange the grilled lemons on the platter with the shrimp for a pretty presentation.

1. In a mixing bowl, whisk together the olive oil, lemon juice, garlic, ¼ cup of the oregano, salt, and pepper. Reserve ½ cup of the marinade and combine the remaining marinade and shrimp in a large resealable plastic bag or a large shallow dish. Marinate in the refrigerator for no more than 15 minutes (marinating longer will change the texture of the shrimp).

2. Preheat the grill to medium-low. Place the shrimp on the lightly oiled grill grates and cook for 4 minutes per side, or until opaque, basting frequently with the ½ cup reserved marinade. Garnish with the lemon wedges and the remaining ¼ cup of oregano. Alternatively, you can use a grill pan on the stovetop—but the flavor is much better when the dish is made on the grill.

HOT DOGS WITH
CLASSIC FIXIN'S

Serves 10 to 12

I keep the hot dog setup pretty basic and mostly for the kids, but you can add as many "extras" for topping the dogs as you'd like.

Grill 10 to 12 natural, all-beef Angus hot dogs (I like Oscar Mayer) on all sides until they have grill marks, are plump, and begin to split, 6 to 8 minutes. Transfer cooked hot dogs to a platter, serve with ketchup, yellow mustard, grainy mustard, pickled relish, chopped white onions, and hot dog buns.

BAKED BEANS

Serves 10 to 12

6 applewood-smoked bacon slices, cut crosswise into 1-inch pieces

1 cup chopped sweet onion

3 28-ounce cans Bush's baked beans (original flavor)

¾ cup unsulfured molasses, such as Grandma's brand

¼ cup packed dark brown sugar

⅓ cup apple cider vinegar

½ teaspoon ground ginger

John loves baked beans! So I set out to find a recipe that would make him happy. When we first got married I remember making baked beans with pretty much every ingredient but the kitchen sink. They were so good! But I can't remember how I did it, and I never wrote it down. So this is my new favorite baked bean recipe—it's John-approved! Just be sure you do not use blackstrap molasses by mistake or you will have bitter baked beans! If you don't have a Dutch oven, start this recipe in a large pot on the stove and finish by baking in two 13 x 9-inch pans in the oven.

1. Preheat the oven to 350°F.

2. Cook the bacon in a large Dutch oven over medium-high heat until crisp. Transfer the bacon to paper towels to drain. Drain rendered fat from the pan, leaving 4 tablespoons in the pan. Add the onion and cook over medium heat for 5 minutes, or until softened. Stir in the beans, molasses, brown sugar, vinegar, ginger, and bacon and bring to a simmer.

3. Bake for 2 hours, stirring after the first hour, or until dark and bubbly. Let stand 15 minutes before serving.

DAD'S MASHED POTATO SALAD

Serves 10 to 12

6 medium russet potatoes, peeled and cut into 2-inch large chunks

¾ cup (1½ sticks) unsalted butter, cut into small pieces

½ teaspoon kosher salt, or to taste

¼ teaspoon freshly ground black pepper

¼ cup warm milk

1 cup plus 2 tablespoons Miracle Whip

¼ cup yellow mustard

¾ cup finely chopped celery

¾ cup finely chopped onion

2 cups finely chopped sweet pickles

¼ cup sweet pickle juice

When I was growing up, my mom cooked most of the meals. But my dad cooked in a pizza restaurant briefly in college and loves to cook. Now he's the one who does most of the cooking for the two of them. Some of my favorite times have been when they visit and he helps me in the kitchen. He's helped me assemble 12 tarts for Delaney's graduation brunch, made our Thanksgiving dinner, and cooked a few meals for us, too. He makes the best tomato pie I've ever had. And this potato salad rocks! What I love about it, and what I think makes it unique, is that he uses mashed potatoes instead of the more common chunks. The trick is really mixing this potato salad well so that you get a little bit of everything in each bite. I like to chop all the ingredients fine so that you never bite into a big chunk of anything because I love the creaminess of it. If chunky potato salad is more your style, then you might want to use your favorite recipe instead. Potato salad is a very personal thing. But this is my absolute fave! Basically you make mashed potatoes and then add the "salad" stuff.

1. Cover the potato chunks with cold water in a large saucepot. Bring to a boil and cook until the potatoes are fork-tender. Drain and return the potatoes to the pot. Add the butter, salt, and pepper.

½ cup plus
1 tablespoon sugar

5 hard-boiled eggs,
peeled and finely
chopped (see Tip)

2 tablespoons
chopped fresh flat-
leaf parsley

Mash with a potato masher or electric hand mixer (essentially you are making mashed potatoes), adding warm milk as needed until the potatoes are smooth and creamy. You should have a little over 6 cups of mashed potatoes.

2. Add the Miracle Whip, mustard, celery, onion, pickles, pickle juice, and sugar, mixing after each addition. Stir in the eggs until combined. Chill at least 1 hour or make the night before and refrigerate. Sprinkle with the chopped fresh parsley before serving.

Tip: *To hard-boil eggs perfectly so that they don't have the dark ring around the yolk, which is a sign they are overcooked, place eggs in a pan, cover with cold water, bring to a boil, and boil 1 minute. Then take the pan off the heat and cover for 13 minutes. Take the eggs out of the water and put them in cold water. Store them in the refrigerator until you are ready to peel and chop them.*

SWEET CORN ON THE COB

Serves 12

12 ears sweet corn, shucked

1 stick unsalted butter, melted

Kosher salt, to taste

Freshly ground black pepper, to taste (optional)

I usually avoid serving corn on the cob at a party because, well, there's the whole corn-in-your-teeth thing. That's never a good look. But I make an exception for this party. It's just so good and about as all-American as you can get. Buy fresh sweet corn, keep it cold, and cook it within a day or two of purchase. While I like corn hot off the grill, your grill may be a bit crowded at this point, so plain ol' boiled corn makes the most sense and I think it is just as good. But don't overcook it! Pierce the cooked ears with little corn grips if you have them to keep guests' fingers from getting greasy; otherwise have lots of napkins at the ready—and toothpicks . . . lots of toothpicks.

Fill a large stockpot three-fourths full of water. Do not add salt to the water or it will toughen the corn, though a bit of sugar is fine. Cover the pot and bring the water to a boil. As soon as it boils, carefully slip the sweet corn into the water. Cover again, and as soon as the water returns to a boil, in about 3 to 4 minutes, remove the pot from the heat. The corn will be cooked perfectly. Transfer the ears to a platter and brush with the melted butter, and sprinkle with kosher salt (and pepper, if you wish).

RED, WHITE, AND BLUE BERRY SALAD

Serves 10 to 12

2 semitart red apples, such as Jazz or Sweet Tango, cored and diced

1 tablespoon fresh lemon juice

2 pints fresh blueberries

2 pints fresh raspberries

1 quart fresh strawberries, quartered (about 8 cups)

¼ cup chopped fresh mint

2 tablespoons superfine sugar

This red, white, and blue fruit salad is not only a crowd-pleaser, but it is an easy opportunity to let the food be part of the decor. Don't peel the apples before dicing.

Combine the apples and lemon juice in a large bowl, tossing to coat. Add the blueberries, raspberries, strawberries, mint, and sugar, stirring gently to combine.

MOM'S PEACH COBBLER

Serves 10 to 12

For the cobbler:

5 to 6 medium ripe peaches, peeled and sliced

¾ cup sugar

3 tablespoons butter, melted

1 teaspoon baking powder

¼ teaspoon salt

½ cup milk

1 cup sifted all-purpose flour

For the topping:

1 tablespoon cornstarch

1 cup sugar

¼ teaspoon cinnamon

⅔ cup boiling water

Vanilla ice cream

My mom made family dinner for us almost every night of the week. Our dining style was very casual. We passed around the bag of Wonder Bread, had instant iced tea with every meal, and used paper towels for napkins (which I still do most of the time). Mealtime was all about talking and sharing our day. Mom made simple but delicious recipes (her fried chicken is the best!), and I can still remember my older brother leaning back in his chair after the meal, stretching, fully satisfied.

When family got together—aunts, uncles, and cousins—it was always at our house. Mom made food for everyone and there was always plenty to eat. It was especially fun when the weather was nice and we got to have a "weenie roast": Dad would make a fire in the dirt in the yard, cut sticks for skewers, and we would all roast our own hot dogs and marshmallows. Mom would fill out the rest of the menu with foods like we have in this cookout and she would make her delicious peach cobbler, served with vanilla ice cream on the side. This recipe brings back all kinds of memories for me.

Occasionally you get your fresh peaches home and they are not a good texture or flavor. This is especially true when they are out of season. I like to freeze ripe peaches for pies or cobblers when they are in season. But, to add more flavor to underripe peaches, toss one quart of peeled (see peeling instructions in Step 2 below) peach slices with the juice of half a lemon and one-third cup sugar in a large bowl and let macerate for about half an hour. The ascorbic acid from the lemon will prevent the flesh from browning. If you don't have frozen ripe peaches and your fresh peaches are a bust, use canned peaches. My mom has done this many times with good results. Sometimes I like to add a cup of raspberries to the peaches. It's so pretty and tasty.

1. Preheat the oven to 375°F.

2. To peel the peaches, cut an "x" in the bottom of each with a paring knife and drop the peaches in a pot of boiling water for 25 seconds. Transfer the peaches with a slotted spoon to a bowl of ice water. Peel off the skin with a paring knife, beginning from the scored end, and discard. Halve the peaches; pit and slice them lengthwise into ¼-inch slices. Arrange the peaches in the bottom of a 13 × 9-inch baking dish.

3. Combine the sugar, butter, baking powder, salt, milk, and flour in a medium bowl. Pour the batter over the peaches. To make the topping, combine the cornstarch, sugar, and cinnamon together and sprinkle over the top of the batter. It's okay if the batter doesn't cover all the fruit, it spreads during baking.

4. Pour the boiling water evenly over the topping. Bake for 45 minutes, or until browned and bubbly. Serve with a scoop of vanilla ice cream on the side.

"John is a borderline fireworks fanatic!"

BRUSCHETTA BASH

Menu

RED WINE SANGRIA

BRUSCHETTA TOPPINGS

ITALIAN: TOMATO, GARLIC, AND BASIL

GREEK: ROASTED RED PEPPER, FETA, AND OLIVES

SALAD LOVER'S: CHICKEN CAESAR

LATIN FUSION: AVOCADO HUMMUS

THE THREE *B*S: BERRIES, BALSAMIC, AND BASIL

FIRESIDE FAVORITE: S'MORES

Serves 10 to 12

This party just sounds fun, right? A bunch of interesting and tasty toppings on crunchy bread . . . what could possibly be wrong with that? Most everything can be made ahead of time and set out for guests to help themselves. This menu is so versatile—it works any season or any time of day, and it's just as great served inside by the fire as it is outside on the patio.

I can still remember the first time I tasted bruschetta, in a studio in Nashville years ago while making my third record, *Wild Angels.* The caterer for the session arrived with a toaster, sliced French bread, fresh garlic cloves, and a container full of the most amazing concoction of tomatoes, garlic, onions, and basil. She toasted the bread, rubbed it with the garlic clove, and topped it with the mixture. One bite and I was in heaven! She taught me how to make it, and it quickly became a favorite snack in my house.

I regularly make it for my band and crew. We eat a lot of catered and restaurant food on the road, so it's a real treat to have something homemade. I love to take care of people (I may have mentioned that) and feeding them is an expression of love for me. I always make sure my tour bus is outfitted with a cooktop. That way, if catering is bad for a few days in a row, I can make a pot of chili and set up a "soup kitchen" in my bus with the band and crew lined up out the door. It makes me feel good to be able to do that for them when they're away from home. My tour manager, Mark Hively, who has been with me for more than twenty years, is easily my biggest bruschetta fan. He always finds a reason to come to my bus when word gets out that I'm making it.

Over the years I've played around with so many different kinds of toppings, both sweet and savory, most of which I've listed here. So a party centered on a variety of help-yourself toppings arranged beautifully on a buffet seemed fun. Once you prep all the ingredients (and I won't lie, it's a lot to prep!), this is actually a very easy party to host because it is relatively hands-off after guests arrive. The colorful toppings are like eye candy and really all the decor you need. Guests are always ready to dig in once they see how beautiful and tempting the food is.

"I love to take care of people . . . and feeding them is an expression of love for me."

my bruschetta bash playlist

1. "Start Me Up" (the Rolling Stones)

2. "Hard to Handle" (the Black Crowes)

3. "Guitar Town" (Steve Earle)

4. "Stay With Me" (Faces)

5. "Pride and Joy" (Stevie Ray Vaughan)

6. "Walk This Way" (Aerosmith)

7. "Rehab" (Any Winehouse)

8. "Back In Black" (AC/DC)

9. "So Long Ago" (Dave Stewart)

10. "Are You Gonna Be My Girl" (Jet)

WOOD, WHITE, AND BLUE ✚ VARIED HEIGHTS ✚ COLORFUL INGREDIENTS

There are so many ways you can set this party up. Keep it supercasual with toppings and bread set on trays on a big square coffee table with your guests sitting on couches or on the floor. Or set it up as a buffet on a long table with serving bowls set at various heights. You can accent this party to look Italian, Greek, Moroccan, Spanish, or all-American.

This is a great party to hold outdoors when it's warm because, in all honesty, bruschetta can be messy! Most recently, I set this up buffet-style in my living room. Of course one of my kids said, "Oh! I thought there was 'no eating in the living room!' " with her fingers in the air in imaginary quotation marks. But hey, sometimes rules are made to be broken, especially when it's so much fun to do so!

I placed tables in front of the dark-blue curtains that frame the French doors to the backyard, so I let the color of the curtains inspire the decor. I went with dark-blue-and-white-patterned linen napkins and chose serving pieces in wood and white—wooden cutting boards, wooden or white bowls, and white plates—and they really stood out against the deep-blue background. Then I added amber (think whiskey) accents.

Long folding tables are inexpensive and a great investment if you entertain a lot, but if you have a rustic wooden sideboard or table, use it. I do like white tablecloths because I think the food stands out against white, but it's not so good for all the dripping and dropping that happens with this party, so a dark-blue cloth works well. I stuck to white plates but made sure to choose plates that weren't too small, so that guests could try a variety of bruschetta at a time. Plates were stacked with the napkins between them at the end of the table. It's important to label the bowls of toppings so guests know what they're trying. I think it adds visual interest when the bowls of toppings are placed at different heights, so if you have tiered stands, use them. You can also use a small, sturdy box or crate as a riser for platters. Honestly, this is one party where I think you could just skip the extra flourishes like flowers and candles if you want. The food and dishes are decoration enough!

You will need lots of sliced, toasted French bread! Right next to the stacked plates on each table, I placed rustic woven baskets and cutting boards overflowing with crostini. Making the bruschetta should be self-explanatory, but if the bruschetta involved more than a single topping, I went ahead and assembled an example so guests would see how to make their own.

DIAL IT UP

Roasting marshmallows over an open fire is always fun. Sure, you can have guests roast marshmallows on skewers in the fireplace, but it is a lot more fun to create a s'mores station with several different flames for guests to gather around. Simply fill a long planter box or a few buckets with decorative pebbles and nestle Sterno canisters or gel fuel cans in the stones. When it's time for dessert bruschetta, simply light the wicks and let the fun begin.

SANITY SAVER

I'm all about shortcuts as long as they don't impact the quality of the end result. When you look over this menu, feel free to turn to convenience items like prepared dressings, containers of prechopped vegetables from the produce aisle, or even a rotisserie chicken instead of grilling chicken for the Salad Lover's bruschetta topping. There is nothing wrong with saving time—especially if it makes the difference between whether you entertain or not!

COOKING GAME PLAN

TWO DAYS BEFORE THE PARTY

- Slice and toast the French bread; cool and store in resealable plastic bags.

ONE DAY BEFORE THE PARTY

- Mix the Red Wine Sangria and chill.

- Prepare the Greek bruschetta topping, excluding the oregano and parsley, cover, and refrigerate.

- Prepare the Italian bruschetta topping, excluding the basil, cover, and refrigerate.

- Grill and dice the chicken and shred the romaine lettuce for the Salad Lover's bruschetta topping, cover, and refrigerate.

MORNING OF THE PARTY

- Make the strawberry mixture for the Three *B*s bruschetta topping, excluding the basil, cover, and refrigerate.

- Make the Avocado Hummus for the Latin Fusion bruschetta topping, cover, and refrigerate.

- Strain the Red Wine Sangria and arrange the bar with the garnish.

ONE HOUR BEFORE THE PARTY

- Arrange the prepared bread slices on platters and cover.

- Stir the basil into the strawberry mixture for the Three *B*s bruschetta topping and arrange in a serving bowl.

- Stir the oregano and parsley into the Greek bruschetta topping and arrange in a serving bowl.

- Stir the basil into the Italian bruschetta topping and arrange in a serving bowl.

- Arrange the Latin Fusion bruschetta topping in a serving bowl.

- Combine the romaine lettuce, chicken, and dressing for the Salad Lover's bruschetta topping. Shave the Parmigiano-Reggiano for the garnish.

- Arrange the S'mores Bar with toppings, graham crackers, and marshmallows.

RED WINE SANGRIA

Serves 10 to 12

12 dried apricots, cut into slivers

1 cup golden raisins

½ cup brandy

2 cups pomegranate juice

½ cup sugar

⅔ cup triple sec

6 whole cloves

3 blood oranges, cut into ¼-inch slices

1 cup fresh cranberries

4 3-inch-long cinnamon sticks

2 Bartlett pears, thinly sliced

2 750-milliliter bottles fruity red wine, such as Rioja

2 10-ounce bottles club soda, chilled

I like good sangria. It's wine and a cocktail, all in one. Plus there's fruit, so it's healthy, right?

1. In a large saucepan stir together the apricots, raisins, brandy, pomegranate juice, and sugar. Cook over medium-low heat until simmering. Remove from the heat and cool slightly. Add the triple sec, cloves, 1 sliced blood orange, cranberries, cinnamon sticks, pears, and wine, stirring to combine.

2. Refrigerate up to 24 hours. To serve, strain the sangria into a pitcher. Serve it over ice and top with club soda, stirring gently. Garnish with the remaining blood orange slices.

ITALIAN: TOMATO, GARLIC, AND BASIL

Serves 10 to 12

2 12-ounce French baguettes, sliced diagonally into ½-inch slices

6 garlic cloves, 3 halved and 3 minced

8 Roma tomatoes, finely chopped

½ cup white onion, finely chopped

½ cup coarsely chopped fresh basil

1 tablespoon balsamic vinegar

2 teaspoons extra-virgin olive oil

½ teaspoon kosher salt

½ teaspoon freshly ground black pepper

This is the amazing topping I had that first time in the studio. It's hard to beat the combination of tomatoes, basil, and garlic—classic and so delicious.

1. Preheat the oven to 400°F. Place bread slices on an ungreased baking sheet. Bake for 2 to 4 minutes, flipping halfway through, until lightly browned and crunchy outside but still slightly soft in the center. Rub with a garlic half.

2. Combine the tomatoes, onion, minced garlic, and basil in a large bowl. Whisk together the balsamic vinegar, olive oil, salt, and pepper in a small bowl. Stir the balsamic vinegar mixture into the tomato mixture. Spoon the tomato mixture evenly over the toasted bread slices.

Tip: Obviously this party calls for a lot of bread! Look through the recipes and make sure you buy enough bread before you get started. It's easiest to make all the bread at once, ideally the day before. Slice the bread, brush with olive oil, and toast on a cookie sheet in a 400°F oven until the bread is a light golden color and still soft in the middle, 2 to 4 minutes, flipping halfway through.

GREEK: ROASTED RED PEPPER, FETA, AND OLIVES

Serves 10 to 12

2 12-ounce French baguettes, cut diagonally into ½-inch slices

1 cup finely chopped roasted red pepper

½ cup chopped pitted Kalamata olives

½ cup chopped peperoncini

½ cup crumbled feta cheese

1 tablespoon fresh lemon juice

¼ cup fresh oregano leaves, coarsely chopped

¼ cup fresh parsley leaves, coarsely chopped

1 tablespoon extra-virgin olive oil

½ teaspoon kosher salt

½ teaspoon freshly ground black pepper

A Mediterranean take on the classic Italian bruschetta, this version is topped with zesty roasted red peppers, peperoncini, lemon, oregano, and feta . . . I mean, what's not to love? And it's so pretty!

1. Preheat the oven to 400°F. Place the bread slices on an ungreased baking sheet. Bake for 2 to 4 minutes, flipping halfway through, until lightly browned and crunchy outside but still slightly soft in the center.

2. Combine the roasted red pepper, Kalamatas, peperoncini, feta, lemon juice, oregano, and parsley in a medium bowl. Stir in the olive oil, salt, and pepper. Spoon evenly over the toasted bread slices.

SALAD LOVER'S: CHICKEN CAESAR

Serves 10 to 12

2 12-ounce French
baguettes, sliced
diagonally into
½-inch slices

2 8-ounce chicken
breasts

3 cups finely
shredded hearts of
romaine (1 to
2 hearts)

⅓ cup bottled Caesar
dressing

8 ounces Parmigiano-
Reggiano, shaved

Caesar salad is one of my go-to salad choices. This is a fun take on a Caesar with the crouton used as the base for the salad.

1. Preheat the oven to 400°F. Place the bread slices on an ungreased baking sheet. Bake for 2 to 4 minutes, flipping halfway through, until lightly browned and crunchy outside but still slightly soft in the center.

2. Preheat the grill to medium-high. Place the chicken on the lightly oiled grill grate or grill pan and cook 6 to 8 minutes on each side, until the juices run clear. Remove from the heat and finely chop.

3. Combine the shredded romaine, chopped chicken, and dressing in a medium bowl. Top the toasted bread slices evenly with the salad mixture and top each serving with shaved Parmigiano-Reggiano.

Latin fusion

LATIN FUSION: AVOCADO HUMMUS

Serves 10 to 12

2 12-ounce French baguettes, sliced diagonally into ½-inch slices

2 15-ounce cans of cannellini beans, rinsed and drained

4 Hass avocados, seeded, peeled, and coarsely chopped

1 cup packed cilantro leaves, chopped

⅔ cup fresh flat-leaf parsley, chopped

¼ cup fresh lemon juice

2 garlic cloves, chopped

1 teaspoon cumin

2 teaspoons kosher salt

½ teaspoon freshly ground black pepper

¼ cup extra-virgin olive oil

1 cup queso fresco, crumbled

This take on hummus, with fresh avocado, feels healthy and fresh. If making ahead, press a piece of plastic wrap directly on the surface of the hummus to prevent browning and refrigerate.

1. Preheat the oven to 400°F. Place the bread slices on an ungreased baking sheet. Bake for 2 to 4 minutes, or until lightly browned and crunchy outside but still slightly soft in the center.

2. Combine the beans, avocados, ¾ cup of the cilantro, parsley, lemon juice, garlic, cumin, salt, and pepper in the bowl of a food processor. Pulse 2 to 3 times, or until the mixture is coarsely chopped. Gradually add the olive oil and process until the mixture is creamy. Spread evenly over the toasted bread slices, sprinkle with crumbled queso fresco, and garnish with the remaining cilantro leaves.

THE THREE *BS*: BERRIES, BALSAMIC, AND BASIL

Serves 10 to 12

2 12-ounce French baguettes or ciabatta loaves, sliced diagonally into ½-inch slices

¼ cup (½ stick) unsalted butter, softened

2 tablespoons sugar, plus 1 teaspoon

½ teaspoon ground cinnamon

2 cups finely chopped strawberries (1 16-ounce container)

¼ cup coarsely chopped fresh basil

2 cups honey-flavored cream cheese

¼ cup balsamic glaze

I first discovered this as a brunch recipe. I made it for a brunch and decided it had to be a part of this menu. It's yummy . . . so much depth of flavor! Balsamic glaze or reduction is readily available nowadays in the grocery store where you find vinegars, but it's supersimple to make. Simply bring ½ cup of balsamic vinegar to a boil in a small saucepan, then turn the heat down to low and simmer until the liquid has reduced by half.

1. Preheat the oven to 400°F. Place the bread slices on an ungreased baking sheet. Bake for 2 to 4 minutes, flipping halfway through, or until lightly browned and crunchy outside but still soft in the center.

2. Mix the butter, 2 tablespoons of the sugar, and the ground cinnamon until smooth. Spread the butter/sugar mixture on the bread and put it under the broiler for 1 to 2 minutes, watching closely, until it's brown, like cinnamon toast.

3. Combine the strawberries, the remaining teaspoon of sugar, and the basil in a medium bowl, stirring to combine. Spread the cream cheese evenly on the toasted buttered bread slices and top with the strawberry mixture. Drizzle each serving with ¼ teaspoon of balsamic glaze.

FIRESIDE FAVORITE: S'MORES

Serves 10 to 12

24 large
marshmallows

24 graham cracker
sheets

24 1.5-ounce
chocolate bars

Who doesn't love s'mores??!! This is such a fun way to end the party. Everyone feels like a kid! You can roast these on skewers in the fireplace or create the s'mores bar described on page 221.

1. Thread the marshmallows onto metal skewers. Heat the marshmallows over an open flame until they begin to brown and melt.

2. Break the graham crackers in half and sandwich the chocolate between the cracker and the hot marshmallow. Allow the marshmallow to cool slightly before eating.

RED WINE AND VINYL

Dry & Spicy

COLUMBIA

Langa La TWZ

Menu

WINE **+** CHEESE **+** PANINI PAIRING

PINOT NOIR **+** SAINT ANDRÉ AND BERRIES **+** PESTO PANINI

MALBEC **+** MANCHEGO AND MARMALADE **+** HAM-AND-CHEESE PANINI

CABERNET SAUVIGNON **+** DANISH BLUE AND
GREEN APPLE **+** CHEDDAR CHEESESTEAK PANINI

PORT (BROADBENT) **+** DARK CHOCOLATE CHUNKS AND COFFEE

Serves 10 to 12

I came up with this party several years ago, and it was so much fun. I went to a used-record store and bought cheap vinyl records that I broke in half at home (if you don't want to destroy an LP, find 45s to use instead). I wrote the invitation in metallic ink right on the black vinyl and then popped the record halves into padded envelopes and mailed them to friends. The invite said:

YOU ARE INVITED TO

THE 1ST ANNUAL RED WINE AND VINYL PARTY

PLEASE BRING ONE OR TWO OF YOUR FAVORITE VINYL RECORDS

(WE WILL SUPPLY THE RED WINE)

This party combines two things I love: wine and music. And it was such a great time! The plan was for each guest to bring a favorite vinyl record (preferably a whole side rather than just one song—remember when we listened to records as a whole?), drink good wine, and enjoy delicious food while enjoying one another's company and taste in music. I can say that there was not one lull during the entire night.

Since red wine is another big part of the party theme, I worked with the guy at my local wine shop to pick three wine varietals. I knew I wanted to pair the wines with cheese as well as provide something a little more substantial for my guests to nibble on. We settled on a lively Pinot Noir, a mellow Malbec, and a big Cabernet Sauvignon (words that might also be used to describe some of the song choices of the evening!). With the wines nailed, I talked to the cheese expert at the grocery store and we selected two cheeses for each wine. One ended up on a cheese board with fruit and the other was layered in the panini I prepared to match with each wine. This is the menu we landed on and it was a hit! I know a little bit about wine, but I still have so much to learn, so for this party I relied on the experts. They guided me along, and made what might have been an intimidating process of creating a menu (especially by a nonexpert) very approachable (and delicious!).

my red wine and vinyl playlist

I've chosen vinyl albums that are iconic. Choose any songs off the album, one side, or the whole thing! Up to you!

1. *Band on the Run* (Paul McCartney and Wings)

2. *Goodbye Yellow Brick Road* (Elton John)

3. *Frampton Comes Alive!* (Peter Frampton)

4. *Sgt. Pepper's Lonely Hearts Club Band* (Or any Beatles)

5. *Back To Black* (Amy Winehouse)

6. *A Night at the Opera* (Queen)

7. *Rickie Lee Jones* (Rickie Lee Jones)

8. *Let It Bleed* (The Rolling Stones)

9. *Rumours* (Fleetwood Mac)

10. *Modern Sounds in Country and Western Music* (Ray Charles)

VINYL AND PAPER +
FREE-FORM SETUP + LAID-BACK
WITH AN EDGE

To be honest, I didn't break my neck (or the bank) decorating for this party. The first impression was all about the invitation. If you're lucky enough to have a used-record store where you live, it's probably your best bet for finding cheap old vinyl records. Flea markets and garage sales can be treasure troves, too. Look for records with iconic labels (RCA Victor, Capitol, and Atlantic, to name a few) or quirky, colorful label designs. When you get home, I highly suggest you do a quick Internet search to be sure you haven't stumbled upon a rare find. It would be sad to wreck something valuable! When you do break the records, be careful to keep as much of the label as possible intact on each half. Use a silver or gold metallic Sharpie or a paint pen to write the party details directly on the black vinyl. You will need a large padded envelope to mail the invitations.

After such a memorable invitation, it's really the wine, food, and music that set the tone. Whether I host this at home or invite guests to Blackbird Studio, which John and I opened ten years ago, the setup is always as simple as dimming the lights, lighting lots of candles, and arranging the food and wine thoughtfully. Throw pillows on the floor and low tables are perfect for creating a relaxed atmosphere. Be sure you have a clear path to the food, wine, and turntable so guests don't fall over each other trying to get to the good stuff!

SANITY SAVER

So you aren't playing host and DJ too, make it Open Mic Night. No, guests do not have to be prepared to sing, but do ask each person to take the floor to introduce their song choices when their record is up. Have people explain why they made their selection, what they love and find interesting or meaningful about the artist or music.

Self-serve parties are always the easiest on the host, so I set up individual tables for each wine-and-food pairing. I covered the tables with brown kraft paper and wrote the names of the wines on the paper in black marker with arrows pointing to the bottles. I wrote the names of the cheeses with a few notes about the flavor profiles and origins of each and drew arrows to the cheese boards. I had all the ingredients for each panini prepared and arranged on platters with instructions for assembly written on the kraft paper. Guests layered the bread with the fillings, and took turns using a panini press that was plugged in at the last station. The panini were a delicious and substantial addition to this wine-fueled soiree. It's always a good idea to have pitchers of ice water sitting around, too.

Recently I've seen old 45s used as trays and coasters, albums used as chargers, and the little yellow plastic rpm adapters that go in the center of 45s repurposed as wine tags. You can take this theme as far as you want to go with it.

Because the party theme is a bit nostalgic, break out a Polaroid camera for candid party pics. Encourage guests to take photos throughout the night and then send them home with their favorites. Or collect all the Polaroids at the end of the evening and make individual collages (like the kind on your bedroom wall in high school) to mail to each guest as a "thanks-for-coming" reminder of a great time.

DIAL IT UP

This is a perfect party for a dance floor. If you have the space, use it. Push the furniture and the wine and food tables to the periphery of the room and let the dance party begin! There is an element of surprise to this party, since the music easily can change from funk to bluegrass to a classic polka melody at a moment's notice. That can make a dance floor a pretty funny addition to the evening, especially as the night progresses.

"This party combines two things I really love: wine and music."

COOKING GAME PLAN

ONE DAY BEFORE THE PARTY

- Prepare the caramelized onions for the Ham-and-Cheese Panini; cover and refrigerate.

- Prepare the onions and peppers for the Cheddar Cheesesteak Panini; cover and refrigerate.

MORNING OF THE PARTY

- Wash and arrange the berries for the berries and fruit for cheese pairings on platters or in serving bowls; cover and refrigerate.

- Cook the beef for the Cheddar Cheesesteak Panini; cover and refrigerate.

- Arrange all panini fillings on platters; cover and refrigerate.

AN HOUR BEFORE THE PARTY

- Arrange cheeses and fruits on the table.

- Assemble sandwiches and cut into sixths; arrange on platters for guests to self-serve.

THIRTY MINUTES BEFORE THE PARTY

- Open wines and let them breathe.

FIFTEEN MINUTES AFTER DINNER

- Pour port into glasses, and set out a tray of dark chocolate broken into chunks.

PESTO PANINI

Serves 10 to 12

2 12-ounce ciabatta loaves (about 12 to 14 inches long)

3 tablespoons extra-virgin olive oil

9 ounces goat cheese

6 small tomatoes, thinly sliced

¾ teaspoon kosher salt

½ teaspoon freshly ground black pepper

½ cup prepared pesto

You may have noticed by now that I love tomatoes, basil, and cheese. This is another spin on the Caprese, Margherita, or Tri-colore dishes Italians do so well.

1. Preheat a panini sandwich press.

2. Split the ciabatta loaves in half horizontally, and brush the bottom halves of bread with 1½ tablespoons of the olive oil, spread evenly with the goat cheese, and top with tomato slices. Sprinkle the tomatoes evenly with salt and pepper. Spread pesto evenly on the top halves of the bread. Place the top halves of the bread over the tomatoes and brush the tops with the remaining 1½ tablespoons of olive oil.

3. Place the sandwiches on the panini press and cook until the bread is lightly browned and the cheese is melted. Cut into sixths and serve.

HAM-AND-CHEESE PANINI

Serves 10 to 12

3 tablespoons butter

5 tablespoons extra-virgin olive oil

3 large red onions, thinly sliced

½ teaspoon kosher salt

½ teaspoon freshly ground black pepper

2 12- to 16-ounce sourdough boules

1½ pounds thinly sliced cooked ham

9 ounces thinly sliced or shredded Fontina

¼ cup Dijon mustard

This is like the perfect comforting ham-and-cheese sandwich. The addition of the caramelized onions takes it up a notch.

1. Preheat a panini press.

2. Melt the butter with 2 tablespoons of the olive oil in a large nonstick skillet over medium heat. Add the onions and cook until a deep golden-brown, stirring frequently, about 40 minutes. Stir in the salt and pepper. Remove from the heat.

3. Split the sourdough loaves in half horizontally, and remove a thin layer of the soft crumb of the bread halves to create a hollow space for the ingredients. Brush the bottom halves of the bread with 1½ tablespoons of the olive oil, spread evenly with the caramelized red onions, and top with the Fontina and ham. Spread the top halves of the bread evenly with the Dijon mustard and place on top of the ham and cheese. Brush the tops of the bread with the remaining 1½ tablespoons of olive oil.

4. Place the sandwiches on the panini press and cook until the bread is lightly browned and the cheese is melted. Cut into sixths and serve.

CHEDDAR CHEESESTEAK PANINI

 Serves 10 to 12

7 tablespoons extra-virgin olive oil

2 medium sweet onions, thinly sliced

3 medium green peppers, sliced

½ teaspoon kosher salt

½ teaspoon freshly ground black pepper

2 pounds rib eye steaks, thinly sliced

2 16-ounce French bread boules

12 ounces shredded Cheddar

Men will flock to this panini. It's certainly substantial. Offer some pickled jalapeño slices for those who aren't afraid of heat.

1. Preheat a panini press.

2. Heat 2 tablespoons of the olive oil in a large nonstick skillet over medium heat. Add the onions and green bell peppers, and cook until softened and lightly browned, stirring frequently, about 12 minutes. Stir in the salt and pepper. Remove the onions and peppers from the pan with a slotted spoon.

3. Heat 2 tablespoons of olive oil in the skillet over medium-high heat. Add the steak slices and cook, stirring frequently for 6 to 8 minutes, or until browned.

4. Split the bread in half horizontally, and remove a thin layer of the soft crumb of the bread halves to create a hollow space for the ingredients. Brush the bottom halves of the bread with 1½ tablespoons of the olive oil, then top evenly with the onions and peppers, steak, and cheese. Brush the tops of the bread with the remaining 1½ tablespoons of olive oil.

5. Place the sandwiches on the panini press and cook until the bread is lightly browned and the cheese is melted. Cut into sixths and serve.

TACO FIESTA

Menu

MARTINA MARGARITA

CHILI-ROASTED PEPITAS

GUACAMOLE

SALSA

CLASSIC BEEF TACOS

HOMEMADE TACO SEASONING

SWEET POTATO AND BLACK BEAN TACOS

CONFETTI RICE

CINNAMON ICE CREAM WITH CINNAMON-SUGAR
TORTILLA CHIPS

Serves 10 to 12

I love Mexican food. Well, honestly, the kind of food I like would probably be labeled Tex-Mex more than authentic Mexican, but only because I haven't had a lot of authentic Mexican dishes. I love the spicy, savory flavors of Tex-Mex, and the cheese!

My go-to order in a Mexican restaurant used to be two cheese enchiladas, rice, and beans. That was pretty much what I got every time. In recent years, I've enjoyed experimenting more at some new restaurants in Nashville that have popped up and specialize in interesting taco combinations such as a southern fried chicken taco, a Buffalo chicken taco, a Korean BBQ taco, and a shrimp po'boy BLT taco. Some of them might sound strange, but I promise you, they are so, so good!

I love this taco trend, and so does my oldest daughter, Delaney. For her eighteenth birthday she asked if I would cook at home for eight of her friends and requested that the theme be inspired by our love of tacos. I put a long table in our hallway and decorated it with brightly colored Fiestaware and embellishments like mini sombreros, Day of the Dead decorations, and mini maracas. Then I made a feast and served Delaney and her friends restaurant-style. It was fun for me and special for them—they were so appreciative. Plus I felt good about having them here at home instead of out. I've done this several times since, these days for her college friends! So I am always on the lookout for interesting taco combinations. Two of my favorites are the basis for this Mexican-themed party.

There are so many great Mexican restaurants in L.A. One of the ones we find ourselves going back to time and time again is the original El Cholo on Western. A friend of ours took us there years ago and it's become a tradition for us when we visit. One of our favorites on the menu is their green corn tamale made with mashed fresh corn, sugar, cheese, and green chiles. They are labor-intensive and who wants to labor in the kitchen when a fiesta awaits! So if you want to add tamales to this menu, I recommend you head to your local Mexican restaurant and order up some to serve alongside your homemade tacos. You can also order the green corn tamales from El Cholo year-round at elcholo.com. Tamales freeze well, so I order (or make) extra to keep on hand.

my latin playlist

This playlist comes courtesy of my Cuban friend Raul Malo, the lead singer of the Mavericks. We have known each other for years and even toured together. I did a duet with him called "Feels Like Home" for his album that can also be heard on my album *The Essential Martina McBride*.

1. "La Venia Bendita" (Marco Antonio Solis)

2. "La Charreada" (Linda Ronstadt)

3. "La Pollera Colorada" (Carmen Revero)

4. "Piel Canela" (Edie Gorme y Trio Los Panchos)

5. "Diablo Rojo" (Rodrigo y Gabriela)

6. "El Rey" (Vincent Fernandez)

7. "A Gozar Timbero" (Tito Puente)

8. "La Sitiera" (Omara Portuondo)

9. "Las Tres Huastecas" (Mariachi Cobre)

10. "Bailame" (Gypsy Kings)

LATIN ACCENTS + BRIGHT COLORS + CASUAL SETUP

Latin-themed parties are fun for all because they are so spirited and casual. There's something about the spicy food (and perhaps the tequila) that just makes people loosen up. This is one party where I like to go really colorful. There are so many places to find Latin-inspired accents for decorating, starting with local Mexican markets (or a few clicks online). I love the look of colorful Mexican blankets on the tables, Mexican prayer candles (available in the international aisle of many supermarkets) scattered about, and bright dishes like Fiestaware or those colorful metallic tumblers from the 1950s for drinks.

I've ordered maracas online and painted guests' names on them, then crossed the handles of each pair on top of the dinner plate to create unique place cards and party favors rolled into one. Big baskets of chips, salsa, and guacamole are easy to throw together and always crowd-pleasers. I place small bowls of cut limes on the table for decoration and for squeezing on food or into drinks. Piñatas make colorful centerpieces and I think the Día de los Muertos, or Day of the Dead, accents are so interesting and beautiful with all the flowers and deep colors. Take the theme as far as you want to go with it.

I've set this party up both indoors and out. John usually takes on margarita duties while I finish up the food. Sometimes I'll ask him to serve the margaritas outside and then have guests wander in for dinner (or if it gets too chilly after dark). Because spicy Latin food and icy margaritas just seem made for warmer months, I host this fiesta most often in summer.

As I've said before, these menus and ideas are just meant to be a jumping-off point, inspirations for you. There are all kinds of ways to do up this party. You can serve one or both of the tacos listed here or find a great gooey, cheesy enchilada or Mexican casserole recipe if the weather is a bit chillier or you want to take a more hands-off approach. With this menu, it's easiest to set up a make-your-own-taco bar. You can include seasoned ground beef or chicken if you think your guests' tastes run a little

more traditional. If you go the enchilada or casserole route, you might prefer a seated, plated dinner setup with the chips, guac, and salsa served during margarita hour, and then plated food for the last two courses. Sometimes a family-style approach—just putting everything out on platters with big bowls of rice and beans on the table works best. How the evening flows really comes down to your personal style and tastes. As long as the conversation is lively, the music fun, and the food tasty, you can't go wrong any way you set it up.

DIAL IT UP

I love the strolling mariachis in Mexican restaurants. The music is so interesting and rich. For a special occasion, or if your budget allows, hire a local mariachi band to come play early on during the margarita hour of the party. I've done that before and it was a huge hit! It really kicks things off and sets the mood for the evening. *Olé!*

SANITY SAVER

I'm all for streamlining party prep and making things as easy as possible. There is no shame in turning to store-bought salsa and guacamole. Find a salsa you like and stock up. If you have time, stir in a little freshly chopped cilantro or diced jalapeño before serving to freshen it up. While you're grabbing salsa at the market, get a couple of different kinds—a chunky traditional salsa as well as a mango salsa for a nice variety. Dump them in pretty bowls, sprinkle a little chopped cilantro on top, and you're good to go!

If you want something more authentic than commercial chips, grab some from your favorite local Mexican restaurant; just make sure they are fresh. If you get to the store and all they have are rock-hard unripened avocados, grab some Wholly Guacamole or guac from the deli counter and dress it up with diced tomatoes, onions, chopped cilantro, and lime to make it chunky and extra delicious. Remember, you don't have to do it all! You just need to do it!

"Remember, you don't have to do it all! You just need to do it!"

COOKING GAME PLAN

THREE DAYS BEFORE THE PARTY

- Juice the limes for the Martina Margarita mixture and refrigerate.

- Mix the cinnamon into the ice cream and freeze.

- If using tequila-filled lime halves, prepare them and freeze.

- Make the Chili-Roasted Pepitas and store in an airtight container.

TWO DAYS BEFORE THE PARTY

- Make the Taco Seasoning.

- Make the Salsa; cover and refrigerate.

- Make the Chipotle Cream sauce for the Sweet Potato and Black Bean Tacos.

- Roast the corn on the grill for the Confetti Rice; remove the kernels from the cobs, cool, cover, and refrigerate.

ONE DAY BEFORE THE PARTY

- Combine the Martina Margarita mixture and chill.

- Chop the onion, cilantro, and jalapeños for the Guacamole and refrigerate.

- Chop the ingredients, rinse and drain the black beans, and shred the cheese for the Sweet Potato and Black Bean Tacos. Cover and refrigerate.

- Place the dessert bowls in the refrigerator to chill.

- Bake the Cinnamon-Sugar Tortilla Chips, cool, and store in an airtight container.

MORNING OF THE PARTY

- Prepare the glasses for the Martina Margaritas by salting the rims.

- Cut lime wedges to garnish the Martina Margaritas.

- Chop the vegetables for the Confetti Rice.

TWO HOURS BEFORE THE PARTY

- Wrap the tortillas in foil packets if warming on the grill or in the oven.

ONE HOUR BEFORE THE PARTY

- If serving tortilla chips, arrange them in baskets.

- Cook the rice for and complete the Confetti Rice.

- Make the filling for the Classic Beef Tacos and keep warm.

THIRTY MINUTES BEFORE THE PARTY

- Make the sweet potato mixture for the Sweet Potato and Black Bean Tacos and roast.

FIFTEEN MINUTES BEFORE THE PARTY

- Warm the packets of corn tortillas on the grill or in the oven, and keep them warm.

MARTINA MARGARITA

Serves 10 to 12

2¼ cups reposado or añejo tequila

2¼ cups fresh lime juice (about 24 limes)

1½ cups simple syrup (see Note) or agave nectar

1 cup kosher salt for rims

3 limes, cut into wedges, for garnish

Orange bitters, such as Fee Brothers or Angostura (optional)

I like to serve margaritas in nontraditional margarita glasses. But there is something fun and kitsch about having the traditional ones. Up to you. I usually use rocks glasses because they are easier to hold, less expected, and don't spill as easily . . . an important consideration after one or two. I like to salt only half of the rim, since some people like salt and some don't. This makes it easy and you don't have to keep asking guests their preference. I prefer a margarita on the rocks, but for easy frozen margaritas, mix 1 can Bacardi Frozen Margarita Mixer with tequila and ice as directed on the can. They are supereasy and yummy! You can make a big batch and even add fresh strawberries if you fancy a strawberry margarita. I'm picky about one thing, though: Too many mixes just taste like SweeTarts. And they are that weird neon-green color. No thank you! Fresh lime juice makes a huge difference.

1. Combine the tequila, lime juice, and simple syrup in a large pitcher without ice. Chill at least 4 hours.

2. Place the kosher salt in a small shallow bowl or plate. Wet the rims (or just one side for salt on half) of the serving glasses by rubbing with the lime wedges. Lightly press the rim of each glass into the salt while slowly turning the glass so that only the outer edge is covered.

3. Fill a cocktail shaker with ice, top off with the *stirred* tequila mixture, add 3 dashes of orange bitters to each serving, if desired, and give it a few shakes. Pour over ice in glasses, and garnish with lime wedges.

Note: Make simple syrup by boiling equal parts sugar and water in a small saucepan just until the sugar has dissolved. Let cool and transfer the syrup to a lidded glass jar. It will keep in the refrigerator up to one month.

Tip: For a fun addition, make floaters by hollowing out lime halves and filling them about three-fourths full with tequila, either a reposado or an añejo (use a great sipping tequila). Set the lime halves in a 12-cup muffin tin for easy filling and then pop them in your freezer to freeze the limes and get the tequila ice-cold for serving.

TEQUILA 101

Tequila is distilled liquor made from the juice of the blue agave plant (the same cactus that gives us the popular natural sweetener agave nectar). Varieties of tequila abound. There is the clear tequila plata (often referred to as blanco, white, or silver); the popular amber-colored tequila reposado, which is aged like wine in oak barrels for less than one year; tequila oro (gold), a less expensive blend of blanco with caramel coloring added. And then there is the smoky tequila añejo, aged for a minimum of one year and prized by tequila lovers and sippers. Personally, I like Patrón Silver for margaritas, but it's nice to understand the offerings so you can choose the variety that suits your tastes and particular cocktail.

CHILI-ROASTED PEPITAS

To make Chili-Roasted Pepitas, preheat the oven to 350°F. Combine 2 cups hulled pumpkin seeds (pepitas) and 2 tablespoons melted butter in a medium bowl with 1½ teaspoons chili powder, 1 teaspoon kosher salt, ½ teaspoon ground cumin, and ⅛ teaspoon ground cayenne pepper, tossing well to coat with the butter and spices. Spread the pepitas in a single layer on a 17 × 13-inch rimmed baking sheet and roast for 10 to 15 minutes, shaking the pan once halfway through. Cool to serve or store up to 1 week in an airtight container. Makes 2 cups.

GUACAMOLE

Serves 10 to 12

½ cup finely chopped white onion

2 jalapeño peppers, seeded and chopped (optional)

⅓ cup fresh lime juice (about 3 to 4 limes)

¼ cup chopped fresh cilantro

2 teaspoons kosher salt

1 teaspoon freshly ground black pepper

½ teaspoon ground cumin

7 ripe Hass avocados

1 cup seeded and diced Roma or beefsteak tomato

This guac is AMAZING! It's really balanced and nice. This recipe makes a ton of guacamole. Typically, 2 large avocados yield about 2 cups mashed avocado, so scale accordingly.

1. In a large bowl, combine the onion, jalapeño (if using), lime juice, cilantro, salt, pepper, and cumin. Mash the mixture with the tines of a fork and stir well.

2. Halve the avocados and throw away the pits. Scoop the flesh into the bowl and mash with the tines of a fork until mixed, leaving some small chunks (or mash until it's creamy, if that's your preference). Gently fold in the diced tomato until combined.

Tip: *Don't be afraid of jalapeños. The heat is in the seeds and membranes, so if you remove them (along with the white pithy ribs running up the inside), you will be left with just a flavorful pepper. Ideally, use gloves when handling chilies (or wash your hands thoroughly after you prep them). And whatever you do, do not scratch, rub, or otherwise go anywhere near your eyes before washing your hands! I learned this the hard way!*

The 411 on avocados: Get them at least a day or two before the party because it can be difficult to find perfectly ripe ones. I'd much rather find underripe ones and let them ripen on the counter than find overripe ones that are brown by the time I'm ready to make the guacamole. If you find your avocados are hard as rocks the night before the party, place them whole in a paper bag with a banana or tomato, close tightly, and leave on the counter overnight. This traps the ethylene gas from the other fruit and speeds the ripening process. Once cut, sprinkle avocado flesh with lemon or lime juice to prevent browning. This is best made right before guests arrive.

SALSA

Serves 10 to 12

8 medium ripe beefsteak or heirloom tomatoes, seeded and diced

2 4½-ounce cans of diced green chilies

2 4¼-ounce cans of chopped black olives

1 bunch scallions, thinly sliced

5 tablespoons vegetable oil

2 tablespoons white wine vinegar

2 garlic cloves, minced

1 teaspoon finely chopped fresh oregano or ½ teaspoon dried

1 teaspoon finely chopped fresh basil or ½ teaspoon dried

1½ teaspoons kosher salt

½ teaspoon freshly ground black pepper

I love fresh salsa! It keeps forever and makes a great low-fat snack to have on hand. This recipe came from an old, battered, food-stained, and much-loved cookbook my mother-in-law, Flavia McBride, gave me for a wedding present. It's from the Junior League of Wichita, Kansas, and it was my go-to cookbook for many years. This salsa has a bit of a Mediterranean flavor with black olives and oregano . . . but it's sooooo tasty and different!

Combine the tomatoes, chilies, olives, scallions, vegetable oil, vinegar, garlic, oregano, basil, salt, and pepper in a bowl and chill at least 2 hours. Serve with tortilla chips.

CLASSIC BEEF TACOS

Serves 10 to 12

2 tablespoons olive oil

2 small red onions, chopped (about 1½ cups)

3 pounds ground beef

2 tablespoons Homemade Taco Seasoning (page 273)

One 14.5-ounce can fire-roasted diced tomatoes, drained

2 15.5-ounce cans chili beans (or 1½ cans refried beans)

Taco shells or flour tortillas

Garnishes:

Shredded lettuce, sliced scallions, sliced black olives, cilantro leaves, salsa, sour cream, shredded Monterey Jack, or crumbled Queso Fresco

Crispy tacos or soft, this back-to-basics beef filling is always a crowd pleaser. Substitute ground turkey if you wish. The beans hold the mixture together.

1. Heat the olive oil in a large Dutch oven over medium-high heat. Add the onion and saute 4 to 5 minutes until softened. Add the ground meat, breaking up with the back of a wooden spoon, and brown 5 to 8 minutes. Drain off excess fat.

2. Add the Taco Seasoning to the meat, stirring to incorporate, and cook 2 minutes to toast the spices and bring out the flavors. Add the tomatoes and beans, reduce the heat to low, and cook 5 minutes more. Mash the beans with the back of a fork (or just use refried beans instead). Serve in taco shells or atop warm flour tortillas with an assortment of garnishes alongside.

HOMEMADE TACO SEASONING

3 tablespoons chili powder

4½ teaspoons ground cumin

¾ teaspoon garlic powder

¾ teaspoon onion powder

1½ teaspoons paprika

¾ teaspoon crushed red pepper flakes

¾ teaspoon dried oregano

2½ teaspoons sea salt (more or less to taste)

1½ teaspoons black pepper

Spice blends are a no-brainer to make, but a big timesaver in the kitchen. Since spices lose flavor over time, making your own blends allows you to make just what you'll use in the near future and tweak the flavors to suit your personal taste.

1. In a small bowl, mix all ingredients and store in an airtight container. (Or you can mix it in the container you are going to store it in—just give it a shake!)

2. Add 2 to 3 tablespoons of this mixture plus ½ to ¾ cup of water to one pound of cooked meat of your choice. Simmer over medium heat, stirring frequently until there is very little liquid left in the pan. Add more spice, to taste.

3. Serve with your favorite taco topping! I recommend lots of sour cream, fresh salsa, guacamole, lettuce, cheese, and tomato.

SWEET POTATO AND BLACK BEAN TACOS

Serves 10 to 12

3 tablespoons vegetable oil

2 white onions, diced

2 large poblanos or Anaheim green chilies, seeded and diced

4 cloves garlic, minced

3 teaspoons kosher salt

2 medium sweet potatoes, peeled and cut into ½-inch dice

24 6-inch corn tortillas

2 cups black beans, rinsed and drained

½ teaspoon freshly ground black pepper

4 cups (12 ounces) shredded Oaxaca or Monterey Jack cheese

Chipotle Cream Sauce (recipe follows)

Pico de gallo (see Note)

I stumbled upon this recipe in O, the Oprah Magazine and it quickly became one of our favorite tacos (thanks, Oprah!). The original recipe suggests serving the tacos "dorado-style," which involves topping the tortillas with cheese and toasting them in a skillet so that the cheese melts before you add the other fillings. That's not an easy undertaking for a party (though if you're whipping these up for a simple family supper, I recommend the method—it's delicious!), so I adapted the serving method. The key is to make sure the tortillas and filling are hot so that the cheese melts a bit when it hits the taco.

1. Preheat the oven to 400°F.

2. Heat a large ovenproof cast-iron skillet over medium-high heat. Add 1 tablespoon of the oil to the pan, then the onions and poblanos. Cook until softened and lightly caramelized, about 5 minutes. Stir in the garlic and 1 teaspoon of the salt. Add the sweet potatoes with the remaining 2 tablespoons oil and 2 teaspoons salt to the pan and stir well to coat with the oil. Cook, stirring, 1 minute, then transfer the pan to the oven and roast for 15 minutes, or until the sweet potatoes are fork-tender. Check after 10 minutes.

3. Line a large microwave-safe casserole dish (with a lid) with a dampened clean kitchen towel. Place 12 tortillas on top of the towel

in the dish and wrap the edges of the towel over to cover the tortillas. Cover the dish with the lid and microwave at 50 percent power for 4 minutes. Let stand for 2 to 3 minutes. Serve the hot tortillas directly from the casserole dish on the serving table or transfer them to a restaurant-style tortilla warmer. Repeat the process with the remaining tortillas as needed.

4. Remove the skillet from the oven and stir in the black beans and pepper to warm the beans through. Set up the taco bar so that guests can grab a hot tortilla, top it with a sprinkling of cheese, the hot sweet potato mixture, a drizzle of chipotle sauce, and a spoonful of pico de gallo.

Note: Basic pico de gallo is a salsa fresca, or uncooked salsa, composed of chopped ripe tomatoes (not canned), chopped white onion, minced jalapeño, and chopped cilantro in proportions that suit your taste (though the tomato typically predominates). Season the mixture with salt and fresh lime juice to taste. Variations might include raw chopped garlic, scallions, radish, jicama, or even cucumber.

CHIPOTLE CREAM SAUCE

Makes ¾ cup

If the chipotle sauce is too spicy for your taste, add more mayonnaise.
Use any extra sauce on sandwiches, grilled corn, or roasted vegetables.

1 to 2 canned chipotles in adobo sauce

1½ cups mayonnaise

Juice of 2 limes

1 teaspoon kosher salt

Place the chipotles, mayonnaise, lime juice, and salt into a blender and blend until smooth.

CONFETTI RICE

3 tablespoons extra-
virgin olive oil

1 medium onion,
finely chopped

1 to 2 garlic cloves,
smashed

1 red bell pepper,
seeded and chopped

1½ cups diced
zucchini

½ medium jalapeño
pepper, seeded and
chopped (optional)

3 cups long-grain
white rice

8 ears fresh yellow
corn, or 6 cups frozen

Kosher salt

Freshly ground black
pepper

1 teaspoon ground
cumin

6 cups chicken stock

2 tomatoes, seeded
and diced

½ cup chopped fresh
cilantro

I like to dice the zucchini, red pepper, tomatoes, and jalapeño pretty small. It's nice and looks like confetti, hence the name.

1. Heat the oil in a heavy, large saucepan over medium-high heat. Add the onion and cook, stirring often until soft and translucent, about 4 minutes. Add the garlic and cook until fragrant, 1 minute, being careful not to let it burn.

2. Add the bell pepper, zucchini, and jalapeño, if using, and sauté until the vegetables just begin to soften, about 4 minutes.

3. Add the rice and corn and sauté 1 minute, stirring constantly to toast the rice and coat with oil. Sprinkle with 1 teaspoon each of the salt and pepper, and the cumin. Pour in the chicken stock, raise the heat to high, and bring to a boil. Reduce the heat to low, cover, and cook until the rice is tender, 18 to 20 minutes.

4. Fluff the rice with a fork and carefully fold in the diced tomatoes and the cilantro. Season with additional salt and pepper to taste.

CINNAMON ICE CREAM WITH CINNAMON-SUGAR TORTILLA CHIPS

Serves 10 to 12

For the cinnamon ice cream:

1 gallon vanilla ice cream

¼ cup ground cinnamon

For the cinnamon-sugar tortilla chips:

5 8-inch flour tortillas

3 tablespoons sugar

2 tablespoons ground cinnamon

Mint sprigs (optional)

It's always great to have a little something sweet at the end of a meal. Especially when it's this easy! You can make the cinnamon ice cream ahead and the tortilla chips the day before.

1. Preheat the oven to 400°F. Line two large 17 × 13-inch baking sheets with parchment paper.

2. Let the ice cream stand at room temperature for 10 to 15 minutes to soften. Transfer the ice cream to a large mixing bowl and gently stir the ground cinnamon into the ice cream until mixed but slightly marbled. Return the ice cream to the original container and freeze.

3. Cut each tortilla into 8 triangles. Place the triangles on the prepared baking sheets and lightly spray with cooking oil. Combine the sugar and cinnamon and sprinkle half the mixture over the prepared tortillas. Turn the tortillas over and repeat the process using the remaining cinnamon-sugar. Bake in the preheated oven for 4 minutes, turn, and bake for 4 minutes more.

4. Scoop the ice cream into chilled bowls and serve it garnished with 3 cinnamon-sugar tortilla chips.

endnote

My party inspiration comes from everywhere. As I do with a cover of a song, I might riff on a common party theme or expand on an idea that started from a single recipe I simply wanted to try or share with others. I love scrolling through images on Pinterest or flipping through the pages of cookbooks and magazines. Many of the ideas I share with you here are built upon the fun things I've pinned, scanned, torn from magazines, or gotten from family and friends. I hope you'll find inspiration from the ideas in this book and use them as a jumping-off point for creating your own unique twists on these themes . . . and share them with me, too!

acknowledgments

Just like making an album, a lot goes into making a book like this a reality and so there are many people to thank!

Amy Bendell, Paige Hazzan, Lisa Sharkey, and the team at HarperCollins: Thank you for believing in me and for caring so much about this book. It's been a treat working with you.

Katherine Cobbs: Thank you for getting and keeping me organized, which is no small feat, for your invaluable insight into the process, and your great ideas along the way.

Thanks to: Jason Wallis and his assistant Eric Chapman for the beautiful photographs and for being so quick! (I hate long photo shoots). Chantal Lambeth and Lauren Lapenna for making all the food look so yummy (it tasted yummy too!), Katherine Tucker and her assistant Prissy Lee for all the fun props and making every shot so inviting and stylish, Catherine Steele for testing all the recipes and making sure they were ready, perfect, and tasty.

Thanks to Simon Green, Cait Hoyt, and Rod Essig at CAA for your enthusiasm and for pitching my idea in the first place. To Clint, Brandon, Mike, Matt, Buffy, Nate, and everyone at Morris Management for encouraging me to make this dream a reality.

To my husband and girls, John, Delaney, Emma, and Ava.: Thanks for tasting all the "experiments" and for understanding when I was focused on writing and behind a computer a few hours each day. Also for lending your stories and being such good sports about the photo shoot!

To my family and friends…thanks for letting me use your recipes and your stories. You all have shaped my life and helped make it worth writing about.

To my glam squad (and longtime friends) Earl Cox and Mary Beth Felts: Thanks for glamming me up! Lord knows I need it! Thanks to Renee Laher for the great style. Thanks also to Ali Benner for all your help with the photo shoot…you know where everything is and we'd be lost without you!

Thanks also to all the chefs, cookbook authors, bloggers, and pinners who have been an inspiration to me… I hope to inspire someone else in the same way.

party log and guest book

Party Name: _____ Date: _____

Menu: _____

_____

_____

Guest Book:

_____

_____

_____

_____

_____

_____

_____

_____

_____

_____

_____

Party Name: _____   Date: _____

_____

Menu: _____

_____

_____

Guest Book:

_____

_____

_____

_____

_____

_____

_____

_____

_____

_____

_____

_____

_____

_____

Party Name: _____ Date: _____

_____

Menu: _____

_____

_____

Guest Book:

_____

_____

_____

_____

_____

_____

_____

_____

_____

_____

_____

_____

_____

_____

Party Name: _____   Date: _____

_____

Menu: _____

_____

_____

Guest Book:

_____

_____

_____

_____

_____

_____

_____

_____

_____

_____

_____

_____

_____

_____

Party Name: _____   Date: _____

_____

Menu: _____

_____

_____

Guest Book:

_____

_____

_____

_____

_____

_____

_____

_____

_____

_____

_____

_____

_____

_____

Party Name: _____ Date: _____

Menu: _____

_____

_____

Guest Book:

_____

_____

_____

_____

_____

_____

_____

_____

_____

_____

_____

_____

_____

_____

Party Name: _____   Date: _____

_____

Menu: _____

_____

_____

Guest Book:

_____

_____

_____

_____

_____

_____

_____

_____

_____

_____

_____

_____

_____

_____

_____

universal conversion chart

Oven temperature equivalents

250 °F = 120 °C

275 °F = 135 °C

300 °F = 150 °C

325 °F = 160 °C

350 °F = 180 °C

375 °F = 190 °C

400 °F = 200 °C

425 °F = 220 °C

450 °F = 230 °C

475 °F = 240 °C

500 °F = 260 °C

Measurement equivalents

Measurements should always be level unless directed otherwise.

$\frac{1}{8}$ teaspoon = 0.5 mL

$\frac{1}{4}$ teaspoon = 1 mL

$\frac{1}{2}$ teaspoon = 2 mL

1 teaspoon = 5 mL

1 tablespoon = 3 teaspoons = $\frac{1}{2}$ fluid ounce = 15 mL

2 tablespoons = $\frac{1}{3}$ cup = 1 fluid ounce = 30 mL

4 tablespoons = $\frac{1}{4}$ cup = 2 fluid ounces = 60 mL

$5\frac{1}{3}$ tablespoons = $\frac{1}{3}$ cup = 3 fluid ounces = 80 mL

8 tablespoons = $\frac{1}{2}$ cup = 4 fluid ounces = 120 mL

$10\frac{2}{3}$ tablespoons = $\frac{2}{3}$ cup = 5 fluid ounces = 160 mL

12 tablespoons = $\frac{3}{4}$ cup = 6 fluid ounces = 180 mL

16 tablespoons = 1 cup = 8 fluid ounces = 240 mL

resources

CrateandBarrel
CrateandBarrel.com

Pottery Barn
Potterybarn.com

West Elm
Westelm.com

Birdkage
Birdkagestyle.com

Cody Foster
Codyfosterandco.com

At Home Furnishings
athome-furnishings.com

Table Matters
table-matters.com

Lenox Corporation
Lenox.com

Kobenstyle
Kobenstyle.com

Tastemotions by Pestritu George Valentin
www.tastemotions.com

index

NOTE: Page references in *italics* indicate photographs.